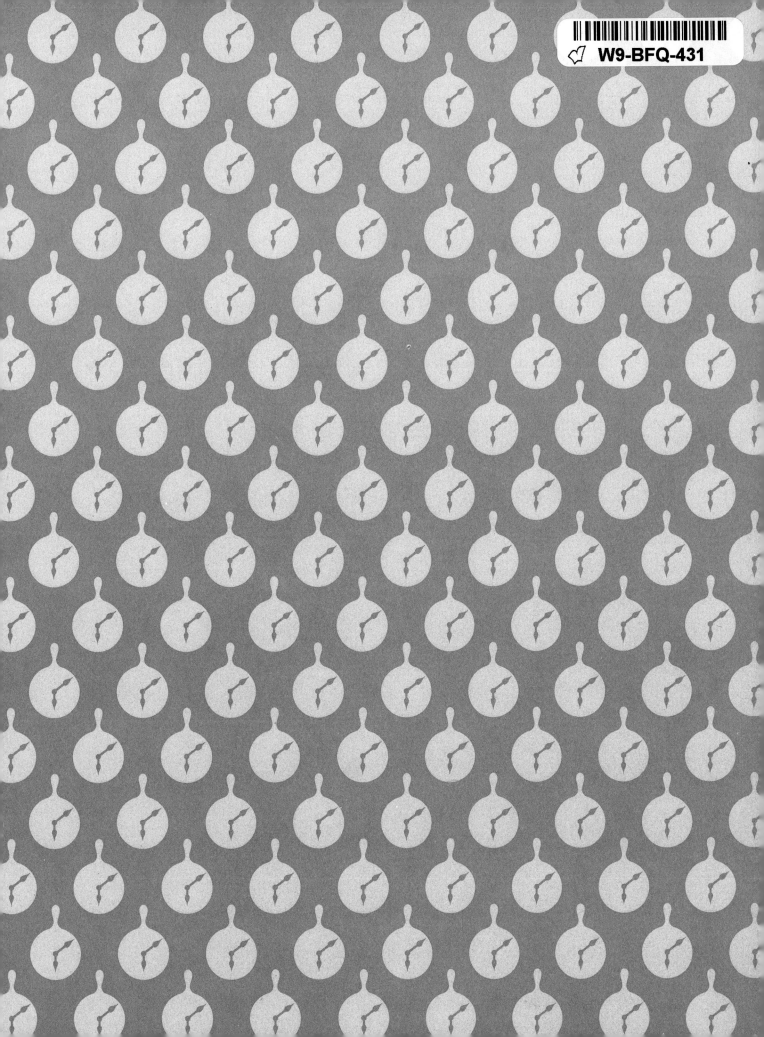

Great Meals in Minutes was created by
Rebus, Inc.
and published by Time-Life Books.

Rebus, Inc.

Publisher: Rodney Friedman
Editorial Director: Shirley Tomkievicz

Editor: Marya Dalrymple
Art Director: Ronald Gross
Senior Editor: Charles Blackwell
Food Editor and Food Stylist: Grace Young
Photographer: Steven Mays
Prop Stylist: Cathryn Schwing
Staff Writer: Alexandra Greeley
Associate Editor: Bonnie J. Slotnick
Editorial Assistant: Ned Miller
Assistant Food Stylist: Karen Hatt
Photography Assistant: Lars Klove
Recipe Tester: Gina Palombi Barclay
Production Assistant: Lisa Young

For information about any Time-Life book,
please write:
Reader Information
Time-Life Books
541 North Fairbanks Court
Chicago, Illinois 60611
Library of Congress Cataloging in Publication Data
Soup & stew menus.
  (Great meals in minutes)
  Includes index.
  1. Soups. 2. Stews. I. Time-Life Books.
II. Title: Soup and stew menus. III. Series.
TX757.S6337 1985   641.8'13   85-16542
ISBN 0-86706-273-8 (lib. bdg.)
ISBN 0-86706-272-X (retail ed.)

Time-Life Books Inc.
is a wholly owned subsidiary of
Time Incorporated
Founder: Henry R. Luce 1898–1967

Editor-in-Chief: Henry Anatole Grunwald
President: J. Richard Munro
Chairman of the Board: Ralph P. Davidson
Corporate Editor: Jason McManus
Group Vice President, Books: Reginald K.
Brack Jr.
Vice President, Books: George Artandi

Time-Life Books Inc.

Editor: George Constable
Executive Editor: George Daniels
Editorial General Manager: Neal Goff
Director of Design: Louis Klein
Editorial Board: Dale M. Brown, Roberta
Conlan, Ellen Phillips, Gerry Schremp,
Donia Ann Steele, Rosalind Stubenberg,
Kit van Tulleken, Henry Woodhead
Director of Research: Phyllis K. Wise
Director of Photography: John Conrad Weiser

President: William J. Henry
Senior Vice President: Christopher T. Linen
Vice Presidents: Stephen L. Bair, Robert A.
Ellis, John M. Fahey Jr., Juanita T. James,
James L. Mercer, Wilhelm R. Saake, Paul R.
Stewart, Christian Strasser

Editorial Operations
Design: Ellen Robling (assistant director)
Copy Chief: Diane Ullius
Editorial Operations: Caroline A. Boubin
(manager)
Production: Celia Beattie
Quality Control: James J. Cox (director),
Sally Collins
Library: Louise D. Forstall

SERIES CONSULTANT
Margaret E. Happel is the author of *Ladies'
Home Journal Adventures in Cooking,*
*Ladies' Home Journal Handbook of Holiday
Cuisine,* and other best-selling cookbooks, as
well as the translator and adapter of Rebecca
Hsu Hiu Min's *Delights of Chinese Cooking.* A
food consultant based in New York City, she
has been director of the food department of
Good Housekeeping and editor of *American
Home* magazine.

WINE CONSULTANT
Tom Maresca combines a full-time career
teaching English literature with writing
about and consuming fine wines. He is the
author of *Mastering Wine a Taste at a Time.*

Cover: Paul Heroux's lobster chowder with
clams and corn, and scallion biscuits. See
pages 96–97.

Great Meals
IN MINUTES

SOUP & STEW
MENUS

TIME-LIFE BOOKS, ALEXANDRIA, VIRGINIA

Contents

Meet the Cooks

YVONNE GILL

Native New Zealander Yvonne Gill, who now lives in Detroit, has had a very diverse career working as a chef, restaurateur, gourmet-food-shop owner, cooking teacher, and lecturer. She has written for *Metropolitan Detroit* magazine and is presently co-publisher of a monthly food newsletter. In 1983, she joined Bormans Inc., a supermarket retailer, as director of specialty foods.

JERRY DI VECCHIO

Born in Kansas and raised in San Francisco, Jerry Di Vecchio—food writer and editor, educator and home economist—has devoted her adult life to good cooking. She is an expert on the foods of the West Coast, and has traveled extensively in Mexico, Europe, and Asia, studying native dishes and their preparation.

DONNA HIGGINS

Home economist Donna Higgins launched her food career as a recipe developer and food stylist in 1960. This led to a position at Del Monte Corporation, where she is director of consumer affairs and services and is responsible for the operation of the company's test kitchens. She is active in several professional organizations, including San Francisco Home Economists in Business and the Society of Consumer Affairs Professionals.

BEATRICE OJAKANGAS

Beatrice Ojakangas first cooked and baked as a 4-H club member in Minnesota. She has worked as a food editor at *Sunset* magazine and has written several books, among them *The Finnish Cookbook*, *Scandinavian Cooking*, and *Great Whole Grain Breads*. She contributes regularly to *Woman's Day*, *Bon Appétit*, and *Gourmet* magazines.

LAURIE GOLDRICH

Laurie Goldrich, who lives and works in Manhattan, trained at the Culinary Institute of America. Her career has included owning a catering business in Vermont, cooking in several leading New York restaurants, and consulting for a major restaurant group. She regularly contributes recipes to national magazines and works as a freelance food stylist.

DAVID RICKETTS

In 1975, David Ricketts left a thriving law practice to pursue a food career. After managing a restaurant on Martha's Vineyard, he apprenticed in a number of professional kitchens, and later worked in the test kitchen of *Food & Wine* magazine. He was an assistant editor of *Cuisine* and is currently the senior associate food editor for *Family Circle*.

CHARLOTTE WALKER

San Franciscan Charlotte Walker runs her own business, Charlotte Walker & Associates, which provides clients with such food-related services as recipe testing, product development, and food styling. She conducts courses at the California Culinary Academy, and is the author of three cookbooks, including *Fish and Shellfish*. She is also president of the San Francisco Professional Food Society.

NANCY VERDE BARR

A specialist in southern Italian cooking, Nancy Barr studied with Madeleine Kamman at Modern Gourmet in Massachusetts and also attended cooking classes given by Marcella and Victor Hazan and Giuliano Bugialli. She has taught cooking in France and at the Chefs Company Cooking School in Rhode Island, and is executive chef to Julia Child on *Good Morning America* and at *Parade* magazine.

PAUL HEROUX

Paul Heroux trained as a professional cook in French restaurants in Massachusetts and Maine, and for two years ran his own catering firm, The Ritz, in Portland. Still living in Maine, he works as an artist and cooks mostly for friends.

Soup & Stew Menus in Minutes
GREAT MEALS FOR FOUR IN AN HOUR OR LESS

Few dishes evoke such a sense of warmth and well-being as a nourishing bowl of soup or stew. Whether it is a clear first-course consommé, a hearty fish chowder, a refreshing chilled vegetable purée, three-bean chili, or a succulent combination of beef, barley, and wild rice, a soup or stew is a welcome lunch or dinner offering at any time of year.

In many ways, soups and stews are very similar. Both are extremely versatile and can be created with almost any foods, including leftovers. In both, the ingredients simmer in liquid for a designated amount of time until they are cooked and blended to savory perfection. Some differences do exist, however: Soups can be served hot or cold, as an appetite-piquing first course, an entrée, or, in the case of some fruit soups, dessert. Stews, on the other hand, are nearly always offered as a main course, and the ingredients in a stew are generally simmered longer and more slowly than those in a soup. Stews also contain less liquid than soups and are often served over rice or pasta.

The origins of soup, according to historians, have been dated from as early as 8000 B.C. in Asia, where cultivated grains were boiled in pottery containers. Later references to soup show up all over the world. In 600 B.C., for example, the Greeks were known to be preparing soups from beans, peas, and lentils. Several centuries later, India's Vedic literature mentions a dish of ground, toasted barley mixed with juices. The Maya are said to have drunk a liquid food made from maize. The word "soup" derives from the Germanic *sop*, which meant bread over which a broth was poured. To "sup" came to mean to eat the evening meal at which this mixture was customarily served.

Although less is known about the origins of stew, it may be assumed that stews have been around since people first began creating mixtures of their favorite meats and vegetables in pots. The Romans are credited with inventing some of the earliest *ragoûts* and fricassees, and by the twelfth century the French were already known for their exquisite stews, among them *blanquettes*, *navarins*, and *matelotes*.

Today, preparing soups and stews may appear to be a time-consuming chore to the cook in a hurry. Indeed, supermarkets offer numerous products that shorten the preparation of these dishes. However, such products often lack the wholesomeness, flavor, and aroma of soups and stews made from scratch. French gastronome Anthelme Brillat-Savarin once said that no woman should marry if she cannot make a soup. He obviously overstated the case, but all modern cooks, male and female, would do well to add soups to their culinary repertoires. As the recipes in this volume show, soups and stews are among the easiest dishes to make, and they do not necessarily require lengthy preparation time or special equipment.

On the following pages, nine of America's most talented cooks present 27 complete menus featuring ideas for appetizer and main-course soups, and for unusual, substantial stews. Many are adaptations of classic recipes from around the world.

Each menu, which serves four people, can be prepared in an hour or less, and the cooks focus on a new kind of American cuisine that not only borrows ideas and techniques from many countries but also values our native traditions. They use fresh produce, and no powdered sauces or other dubious shortcuts. The other ingredients called for (vinegars, spices, herbs, and so on) are all of high quality and usually are available in supermarkets or specialty food stores.

The cooks and the kitchen staff have meticulously planned and tested the menus for appearance as well as for taste, as the accompanying photographs show: The vegetables are brilliant and fresh, the visual combinations appetizing. The table settings feature bright colors, simple flower arrangements, and attractive but not necessarily expensive serving dishes.

For each menu, the Editors, with advice from the cooks, suggest wines and other beverages. And there are suggestions for the use of leftovers and for complementary dishes and desserts. On each menu page, you will find a number of other tips, from an easy method for shredding squash to advice for selecting fresh produce.

BEFORE YOU START

Great Meals in Minutes is designed for efficiency and ease. This book will work best for you if you follow these suggestions:

1. Refresh your memory with the few simple cooking techniques on the following pages. They will quickly become second nature, and will help you produce professional-quality meals in minutes.

Whatever the season, a soup or stew makes a delicious meal for family or friends. For optimum results, fill your stockpot with only the freshest herbs and produce.

7

2. Read the menus before you shop. Each lists the ingredients you will need, in the order that you would expect to shop for them. Many items will already be on your pantry shelf.

3. Check the equipment list on page 14. Good sharp knives and pots and pans of the right shape and material are essential for making great meals in minutes. This may be the time to buy a few things: The right equipment can turn cooking from a necessity into a creative experience.

4. Set out everything you need before you start to cook. The lists at the beginning of each menu tell just what is required. To save effort, always keep your ingredients in the same place so you can reach for them instinctively.

5. Follow the start-to-finish steps for each menu. That way, you can be sure of having the entire meal ready to serve in an hour.

SOUPS IN THIS VOLUME

Although there are perhaps thousands of soup recipes in the world, they can be grouped into a few general categories by their ingredients and preparation techniques. In this volume you will find examples of thin and clear soups, creamy purée soups, compound soups, and chilled soups.

Thin and Clear Soups

These soups are made from chicken, fish, beef, or vegetable stock (see page 10 for complete information on making your own stock) served unclarified, or clarified as bouillons or consommés. Clear soups are often garnished just before serving with eggs, pasta, or vegetables or substantially enriched by the addition of dumplings. On page 31, Jerry Di Vecchio adds scallop balls and shrimp to ginger-spiced chicken soup, and on page 99 Paul Heroux fortifies a clear beef broth with hearty dumplings made from pork, chicken, and crabmeat.

Purée Soups

Characterized by their relatively homogeneous texture and smooth consistency, purée soups are harmonious blends of flavors. Almost any foods can be puréed, singly or in combination, and once puréed, the minute particles stay suspended in the liquid. Some purées require a thickener such as flour or cornstarch to bind the solids and keep them from separating from the liquid. When flour is the thickener, it must be thoroughly cooked to remove the starchy taste and to prevent it from giving the soup a sticky texture.

If the main ingredient of a purée soup is a starch, such as potatoes, dried beans, or lentils, no further thickening agent is required. If you are puréeing a starch in a food processor, you may want to do it in two batches. If you are using a sieve, moisten the starch with a little cooking liquid as you proceed so it does not clog the holes. Beatrice Ojakangas purées potatoes for one of her two chilled soups in Menu 2, page 51, and David Ricketts prepares a puréed yam soup with ham on page 69.

If the basis for your purée soup is vegetables, you can start with fresh vegetables that are young and at their flavor peak, or use whatever vegetables you have left over from earlier meals.

Just before serving, egg yolks, light or heavy cream, milk, or butter are often added to a purée soup to further thicken and enrich it and to give it a desirable velvety appearance. Donna Higgins adds a generous amount of light cream to her broccoli-leek soup in Menu 3, page 45.

Compound Soups

Just as the name implies, compound soups are hearty medleys of ingredients with contrasting tastes and textures. Substantial and nourishing, these dishes are so complete that when they are served with bread and a light salad, they make a meal in themselves. Compound soups resemble stews except that they contain a higher ratio of liquids to solids, and their ingredients are cut into smaller pieces. Many classic dishes and their variations are considered compound soups, among them chowders and gumbos.

Chowders are thick soups often featuring seafood in a milk base. The word "chowder" comes from the French *chaudière*, a three-legged cast-iron pot that sits over a heat source (originally hot coals). The pot was traditionally used for stewing freshly caught seafood with vegetables and seasonings. Today, many chowders still call for seafood, and a true New England chowder always contains salt pork, onions, and potatoes as well. On page 96, Paul Heroux prepares his own chowder variation using lobster, clams, leeks, fennel, and vermouth to produce a delicately aromatic main course. Another chowder-like dish, the French *bourride*, is offered by Yvonne Gill on page 21.

Gumbos are soups made famous by Creole cooks in Louisiana. "Gumbo" comes from the African word *quingumbo*, meaning "okra," and this vegetable continues to be used in most gumbos for its thickening properties. Gumbos evolved as an economical means of using up whatever meat, fish or shellfish, poultry, game, or vegetables happened to be available; therefore, there is no standard gumbo recipe. In general, gumbos are served over rice. On page 61, Laurie Goldrich presents a chicken gumbo that includes okra and spicy Louisiana sausage.

When preparing compound soups, remember that meat and poultry will cook more slowly than vegetables or pasta. Depending on the ingredients you use, add them to the soup in stages to prevent overcooking. David Ricketts does this with his wild rice and sausage soup on page 72, and Nancy Barr also prepares her minestrone in stages on page 90.

Chilled Soups

A cold soup is exceptionally refreshing for a hot-weather meal; it is also good as an appetizer and, in some cases, as a dessert. Cold soups may be chilled versions of hot soups, or they may be soups blended from fresh summer vegetables or fruits that do not require cooking at all.

Thin, clear soups and purée soups lend themselves best to chilling. If you intend to chill a hot purée soup, it should be cooked with little or no butter so that the fat will not solidify upon chilling. Just before serving, you can reblend the purée if necessary to ensure its homogeneity. Chilling may also mute the flavor of a soup, so taste and readjust the seasonings before you serve it. Beatrice Ojakangas serves two chilled purée soups in one bowl on page 51.

STEWS IN THIS VOLUME

Like soups, stews in their infinite variations are popular in virtually every cuisine. Still, all stews are prepared in essentially the same way—that is, the ingredients are simmered in liquid in a lidded container until they are tender and their juices are reduced and thickened. Typically, the meats used in stews are economical tougher cuts that benefit from the tenderizing effect of long, slow cooking. To produce stews in less than an hour for this volume, however, the cooks call for tender cuts of meat that cook through quickly. Vegetables and other ingredients are added at various intervals during the cooking to retain their texture or color. You will find a wide variety of international stews, ranging from a simple Scandinavian-American beef, barley, and wild rice stew prepared by Beatrice Ojakangas on page 54, to more unusual stews, such as Laurie Goldrich's Creole *grillades* on page 58, and Jerry Di Vecchio's crisp pork stew with peanut sauce and cellophane noodles on page 28.

Two other more specialized stews included in this volume are a French *ragoût* and an American chili. A *ragoût*, from the French verb *ragoûter* ("to revive the appetite"), is a sophisticated stew that often includes wine and an intriguing blend of seasonings in the sauce. *Ragoûts* are based predominantly on meat, poultry, or seafood, and sometimes feature vegetables. Yvonne Gill offers a veal *ragoût* with peppers on page 18, which she thickens with *crème fraîche*, and she prepares a *blanquette*, or white *ragoût*, made with poached chicken breasts in her Menu 3 on page 24.

Chili is a type of stew created along the cattle trails of nineteenth-century Texas that has become a staple of southwestern cooking. Although chili began as an all-beef (no beans) dish fired with ground hot chili peppers, today there are as many chili recipes as there are cooks—and many of them contain no beef at all. On page 79, Charlotte Walker prepares a vegetarian chili in which she uses three types of beans.

GENERAL COOKING TECHNIQUES

Sautéing

Sautéing is a form of quick frying with no cover on the pan. In French, *sauter* means "to jump," which is what vegetables or small pieces of food do when you shake the sauté pan. The purpose is to brown the food lightly and seal in the juices, sometimes before further cooking. This technique has three critical elements: the right pan, the proper temperature, and dry food.

The sauté pan: A proper sauté pan is 10 to 12 inches in diameter and has 2- to 3-inch straight sides that allow you

Soup Garnishes

Many soups, particularly those of fairly uniform color and texture, are more appetizing when served with a garnish. A number of the soup recipes in this volume include suggestions for toppings such as fresh herbs, finely cut vegetables, or cream. Here are a few ideas for other attractive finishing touches for your own soup creations. Keep in mind subtleties of flavor and texture, and use a light hand when garnishing a soup.

Croutons: Bread cubes browned in butter or oil complement clear soups, purées, and even more elaborate soups. Try different types of bread, and season the croutons with herbs and spices. On page 59, Laurie Goldrich prepares pumpernickel croutons for a salad; they would also be good on a soup.

Other bread garnishes: Petite squares or triangles of toast—or more elaborate shapes cut with a small cookie cutter—can be floated on the surface of a soup just before serving. For extra flavor, spread the toasts with flavored butter, cheese, or pesto. Small crackers can be used in the same manner.

Popcorn, cereal, nuts: Cheese-flavored popcorn is good with tomato and other puréed vegetable soups. Unsweetened puffed cereal may be used in the same way. Slivered toasted almonds enrich pale, creamy soups.

Making Stock

A good stock is the foundation for most soups and stews in this volume, and is also an excellent base for sauces and gravies. Although canned stock or broth is acceptable to use when you are short on time, homemade stock has a rich flavor that is hard to match. Moreover, canned products are likely to be overly salty. Homemade stock—whether it is chicken, beef, or fish—is not difficult to make. The following pointers will ensure a rich, clear stock, no matter which type you make.

Use a large nonaluminum stockpot or saucepan. Stir the stock as little as possible to prevent clouding. Watch carefully to make sure the stock stays at a simmer but does not boil.

Chicken Stock

Save chicken parts as they accumulate and freeze them. The yellow onion skin adds color; the optional veal bone adds extra flavor and richness.

3 pounds bony chicken parts, such as wings,
   back, and neck
1 veal knuckle (optional)
Yellow onion, unpeeled and stuck with 2 whole cloves
2 stalks celery with leaves, halved
12 peppercorns
2 carrots, peeled and cut into 2-inch lengths
4 sprigs parsley
1 bay leaf
1 tablespoon chopped fresh thyme, or 1 teaspoon dried
Salt

1. Wash chicken parts, and veal knuckle if using, and drain. Place in stockpot with remaining ingredients (except salt) and add 3 quarts cold water. Cover pot and bring to a boil over medium heat.
2. Reduce heat and simmer stock, partially covered, 2 to 3 hours, skimming foam and scum from surface several times. Add salt to taste after stock has cooked 1 hour.
3. Strain stock through fine sieve placed over large bowl. Discard solids. Let stock cool uncovered; refrigerate when completely cool.

Beef Stock

Use marrow bones and an inexpensive cut of beef, such as shin, in roughly equal amounts. If you use beef knuckle, have the butcher saw it into quarters.

2 pounds shin of beef with bone
2 pounds marrow bones, or 1 pound marrow bones and
   1 beef knuckle
1 leek, trimmed (optional)
2 carrots, peeled and cut into 2-inch lengths
3 or 4 stalks celery with leaves, halved
6 to 8 sprigs parsley
1½ teaspoons chopped fresh thyme, or ½ to ¾ teaspoon dried
Large onion, unpeeled
3 cloves garlic, unpeeled (optional)
1 bay leaf
6 whole cloves (optional)

Cooking chicken or beef stock a half hour more or less will not affect its flavor significantly; however, if fish stock is cooked for more than 30 minutes, it may acquire an unpleasant taste. Once cooked, cool the stock as quickly as possible, preferably by placing the pan in a sinkful of cold water. Do not cover it as it cools, and refrigerate it as soon as it has cooled. After several hours of refrigeration, the fat will congeal at the top of the stock; it may be removed or left as a protective covering. At this point, transfer the stock to jars or freezer containers (1-cup sizes are convenient); it will keep for up to three days in the refrigerator and up to three months in the freezer.

8 peppercorns
1½ teaspoons salt

1. Place beef and bones in stockpot and add about 4 quarts cold water, or enough water to cover beef and bones by about 2 inches. Bring stock to a simmer over medium heat, skimming foam and scum from surface as it rises.
2. When scum has almost stopped surfacing, add vegetables, herbs, and seasonings, and return to a simmer. Partially cover pot, reduce heat to low, and simmer stock gently, skimming as necessary, 4 to 5 hours.
3. Taste stock. Reduce further if flavor needs to be intensified, or add water if it has reduced too much and flavor is too strong.
4. Strain stock through fine sieve placed over large bowl. Discard solids. Let stock cool uncovered; refrigerate when completely cool.

Fish Stock

Ask your fish dealer to provide you with some trimmings. You may want to request them a day in advance.

2 pounds fish bones, heads, and tails
½ cup sliced carrots
½ cup sliced onions or shallots
½ cup sliced celery
1 bay leaf
5 or 6 sprigs parsley
8 peppercorns
2 cups white wine (optional)
Salt

1. Remove gills from heads, if necessary. Rinse fish under cold running water and cut or break into chunks.
2. Place fish in stockpot with vegetables, seasonings, and wine, if using. Do not add salt at this point. Add 6 cups cold water if using wine, 8 cups if not. Bring to a boil over high heat. Reduce heat and simmer stock, uncovered, 30 minutes, skimming as necessary. Stock should reduce by about half.
3. Strain stock through fine sieve set over large bowl. If not sufficiently reduced, return strained stock to pot and bring to a boil over high heat. Reduce heat and simmer stock, uncovered, until reduction is complete. Add salt to taste.
4. Let stock cool uncovered; refrigerate when completely cool.

to turn the food and still keep the fat from spattering. It has a heavy bottom that can be moved back and forth easily across a burner.

The best material (and the most expensive) for a sauté pan is tin-lined copper, because it is a superior heat conductor. Heavy-gauge aluminum works well but will discolor acidic food like tomatoes. Therefore, you should not use aluminum if acidic food is to be cooked for more than 20 minutes after the initial browning. Another option is to select a heavy-duty sauté pan made of strong, heat-conducting aluminum alloys. This type of professional cookware is smooth and stick resistant.

Use a sauté pan large enough to hold the food without crowding, or sauté in two batches. The heat of the fat and the air spaces around and between the pieces facilitate browning.

Many recipes call for sautéing first, then lowering the heat and cooking the food, covered, for an additional 10 to 20 minutes. Be sure you buy a sauté pan with a tight-fitting cover. Make certain the handle is long and is comfortable to hold. Use a wooden spatula or tongs to keep food moving in the pan as you shake it over the burner. If the food sticks, as it occasionally will, a metal spatula will loosen it best. Turn the food so that all surfaces come into contact with the hot fat.

Never immerse the hot pan in cold water because this will warp the metal. Allow the pan to cool slightly, then add water and let it sit until you are ready to wash it.

The fat: Half butter and half vegetable or peanut oil is perfect for most sautéing: It heats to high temperatures without burning, yet gives a rich butter flavor. For cooking, unsalted butter tastes best and adds no extra salt.

Some sautéing recipes in this book call for olive oil, which imparts a delicious and distinctive flavor of its own and is less sensitive than butter to high heat. Nevertheless, even the finest olive oil has some residue of fruit pulp, which occasionally will scorch. Watch carefully when you sauté in olive oil; discard any scorched oil and start with fresh, if necessary.

To sauté properly, heat the fat until it is hot but not smoking. When you see small bubbles on top of the fat, lower the heat because the fat is on the verge of smoking. When using butter and oil together, add butter to the hot oil. After the foam from the melting butter subsides, you are ready to sauté. If the temperature of the fat is just right, the food will sizzle when you put it in the pan. David Ricketts sautés spinach in Menu 1, page 67.

Searing

When you sear, you brown the meat without shaking the pan or stirring. Heat the oil until it is very hot, then brown the meat over high heat for a minute or two on each side. A metal spatula is essential, for the meat will tend to stick. Wait until the meat is very brown on one side before you turn it. Yvonne Gill sears cubes of veal for her Menu 1 *ragoût*, page 18.

Stir Frying

The basic cooking method for Chinese cuisine, this fast-cook technique requires very little oil, and the foods—which you stir continuously—fry quickly over very high heat. Stir frying is ideal for cooking bite-size, shredded, or thinly sliced portions of vegetables, fish, meat, or poultry, alone or in combination. Jerry Di Vecchio stir fries *bok choy*, page 29.

Deglazing

This is an easy way to create a sauce for sautéed, braised, or roasted food. To deglaze, pour off all but 1 or 2 tablespoons of fat from the pan in which the food has been cooked. Add liquid—water, wine, or stock—and reduce the sauce over medium heat, using a wooden spoon to scrape up and blend into the sauce the concentrated juices and browned bits of food clinging to the bottom of the pan. Donna Higgins uses this method in her recipe for savory lentil stew, page 38.

Blanching

Also called parboiling, blanching is an invaluable technique. Immerse whole or cut vegetables or other foods for a few minutes in boiling water, then refresh them, that is, plunge them into cold water to stop their cooking and set their colors. Blanching softens or tenderizes dense or crisp vegetables, often as a preliminary to further cooking by another method, such as stir frying. Yvonne Gill blanches green beans in Menu 3, page 24.

Steaming

Steaming is an easy way to cook vegetables and other foods, including desserts. Bring water to a boil in a saucepan. Place the food in a steamer or on a rack over the liquid and cover the pan, periodically checking the water level. Keeping the food above the liquid preserves vitamins and minerals often lost in other methods of cooking. Jerry Di Vecchio steams ginger custards, page 29.

Poaching

You poach meat, fish, chicken, fruit, and eggs in very hot liquid in a pan on top of the stove. You can use water or, better still, beef, chicken, or fish stock, or a combination of stock and wine, or even cream as the poaching liquid. Jerry Di Vecchio poaches scallop balls for her soup, page 31.

Broiling and Grilling

In broiling, the food cooks directly under the heat source. In grilling, the food cooks either directly over an open fire or on a well-seasoned griddle placed directly over a burner. Paul Heroux broils oysters in his Menu 3 on page 101.

Baking

Baking applies to the dry-heat cooking of foods such as casseroles; small cuts of meat, fish, poultry, and vegetables; and, of course, breads and pastries. Some foods are baked tightly covered to retain their juices and flavors; others, such as breads, cakes, and cookies, are baked in open pans to release moisture. Paul Heroux bakes squash on page 102.

Pantry (for this volume)

A well-stocked, properly organized pantry is essential for preparing great meals in the shortest time possible. Whether your pantry consists of a small refrigerator and two or three shelves over the sink, or a large freezer, refrigerator, and entire room just off the kitchen, you must protect staples from heat and light.

In maintaining your pantry, follow these rules:

1. Store staples by kind and date. Canned goods, canisters, and spices need a separate shelf, or a separate spot on a shelf. Date all staples—shelved, refrigerated, or frozen—by writing the date directly on the package or on a bit of masking tape. Then put the oldest ones in front to be sure you use them first.

2. Store flour, sugar, and other dry ingredients in canisters or jars with tight lids. Glass and clear plastic allow you to see at a glance how much remains.

3. Keep a running grocery list so that you can note when a staple is half gone, and be sure to stock up.

ON THE SHELF:

Anchovies
Anchovy fillets, both flat and rolled, come oil-packed, in tins.

Baking powder

Baking soda

Capers
Capers are usually packed in vinegar and less frequently in salt. If you use the latter, you should rinse them under cold water before using them.

Clam juice, bottled
May be substituted for fish stock. Be careful to add it gradually; it is very salty and may need to be diluted.

Cornstarch
Less likely to lump than flour, cornstarch is an excellent thickener for sauces. Substitute in the following proportions: 1 tablespoon cornstarch to 2 of flour.

Flour
all-purpose, bleached or unbleached

Garlic
Store in a cool, dry, well-ventilated place. Garlic powder and garlic salt are not adequate substitutes for fresh garlic.

Herbs and spices
The flavor of fresh herbs is much better than that of dried. Fresh herbs should be refrigerated and used as soon as possible. The following herbs are perfectly acceptable dried, but buy in small amounts, store airtight in dry area away from heat and light, and use as quickly as possible. In measuring herbs, remember that one part dried will equal three parts fresh. Crushing dried herbs brings out their flavor: Use a mortar and pestle or sandwich the herbs between 2 sheets of waxed paper and crush with a rolling pin.
Note: Dried chives and parsley should not be on your shelf, since they have little or no flavor; frozen chives are acceptable. Buy whole spices rather than ground, as they keep their flavor much longer. Grind spices at home and store as directed for herbs.

allspice, whole and ground
basil
bay leaves
Cayenne pepper
cumin
dill
fennel seeds
ginger
marjoram
mustard, whole seeds and powdered
oregano
paprika
pepper
  black peppercorns
  These are unripe peppercorns dried in their husks. Grind with a pepper mill for each use.
  white peppercorns
  These are the same as the black variety, but are picked ripe and husked. Use them in pale sauces when black pepper specks would spoil the appearance.
red pepper flakes (also called crushed red pepper)
rosemary
saffron
  Made from the dried stigmas of a species of crocus, this spice—the most costly of all seasonings—adds both color and flavor. Available powdered or in threads. Use sparingly.
salt
  Use coarse salt—commonly available as kosher or sea—for its superior flavor, texture, and purity. Kosher salt and sea salt are less salty than table salt. Substitute in the following proportions: three-quarters teaspoon table salt equals just under one teaspoon kosher or sea salt.
savory
tarragon
thyme

Honey

Nuts, whole, chopped or slivered
almonds
pecans
pine nuts (pignoli)
walnuts

Oils
corn, safflower, or vegetable
  Because these neutral-tasting oils have high smoking points, they are good for high-heat sautéing.
olive oil
  Olive oil ranges in color from pale yellow to dark green and in taste from mild and delicate to rich and fruity. Different olive oils can be used for different purposes: for example, stronger ones for cooking, lighter ones for salads. The finest-quality olive oil is labeled extra-virgin or virgin.
walnut oil
  Rich and nutty tasting. It turns rancid easily, so keep it in the refrigerator.

Olives
Kalamata olives
  Dark purple almond-shaped Greek olives that have been brine cured and packed in vinegar.
pitted black olives

Onions
Store all dry-skinned onions in a cool, dry, well-ventilated place.
red or Italian onions
  Zesty tasting and generally eaten raw. The perfect salad onion.
shallots
  The most subtle member of the onion family, the shallot has a delicate garlic flavor.
white onions
  Also called boiling onions, these small onions are almost always cooked and served whole.
yellow onions
  All-purpose cooking onions, strong in taste.

Potatoes, boiling and baking

"New" potatoes are not a particular kind of potato, but any potato that has not been stored.

Rice

long-grain white rice

Slender grains, much longer than they are wide, that become light and fluffy when cooked and are best for general use.

Soy sauce

Stock, chicken, beef, and fish

For maximum flavor and quality, your own stock is best (see recipes page 10), but canned stock, or broth, is convenient to have on hand.

Sugar

confectioners' sugar
granulated sugar

Tomatoes

Italian plum tomatoes

Canned plum tomatoes (preferably imported) are an acceptable substitute for fresh.

tomato paste

Sometimes available in tubes, which can be refrigerated and kept for future use after a small amount is used. With canned paste, spoon out unused portions in one-tablespoon amounts onto waxed paper and freeze, then lift the frozen paste off and store in a plastic container.

Vinegars

balsamic vinegar

Aged vinegar with a complex sweet and sour taste

raspberry vinegar

A white wine vinegar infused with fresh berries.

red and white wine vinegars

rice vinegar

tarragon or basil vinegar

White wine vinegars flavored with fresh herbs, they are especially good in salads.

Wild rice

Wines and spirits

Cointreau or other orange-flavored liqueur

red wine, dry

sherry, dry

white wine, dry

Worcestershire Sauce

IN THE REFRIGERATOR:

Basil

Though fresh basil is widely available only in summer, try to use it whenever possible to replace dried; the flavor is markedly superior. Stand the stems, preferably with roots intact, in a jar of water, and loosely cover leaves with a plastic bag.

Bread crumbs

You need never buy bread crumbs. To make fresh crumbs, use fresh or day-old bread and process in food processor or blender. For dried, toast bread 30 minutes in preheated 250-degree oven, turning occasionally to prevent slices from browning. Proceed as for fresh. Store bread crumbs in an airtight container: fresh crumbs in the refrigerator, and dried crumbs in a cool, dry place. Either type may also be frozen for several weeks if tightly wrapped in a plastic bag.

Butter

Many cooks prefer unsalted butter because of its finer flavor and because it does not burn as easily as salted.

Cheese

Cheddar cheese, sharp

A firm cheese, ranging in color from nearly white to yellow. Cheddar is a versatile cooking cheese.

Parmesan

Avoid the pre-grated packaged variety; it is very expensive and almost flavorless. Buy Parmesan by the quarter- or half-pound wedge and grate as needed: 4 ounces produces about one cup of grated cheese.

Coriander

Also called *cilantro* or Chinese parsley, its pungent leaves resemble flat-leaf parsley. Keep in a glass of water covered with a plastic bag.

Cream

half-and-half

heavy cream

sour cream

Eggs

Will keep 4 to 5 weeks in refrigerator. For best results, bring to room temperature before using.

Ginger, fresh

Found in the produce section. Wrap in a paper towel, then in plastic, and refrigerate; it will keep for about 1 month, but should be checked weekly for mold. Or, if you prefer, store it in the freezer, where it will last about 3 months. Firm, smooth-skinned ginger need not be peeled.

Lemons

In addition to its many uses in cooking, a slice of lemon rubbed over cut apples and pears will keep them from discoloring. Do not substitute bottled juice or lemon extract.

Limes

Mayonnaise, homemade, or commercial

Milk

Mint

Fresh mint will keep for a week if wrapped in a damp paper towel and enclosed in a plastic bag.

Mustard

The recipes in this book call for Dijon mustard.

Parsley

The two most commonly available kinds of parsley are flat-leaved and curly; they can be used interchangeably when necessary. Flat-leaved parsley has a more distinctive flavor and is generally preferred in cooking. Curly parsley wilts less easily and is excellent for garnishing. Store parsley in a glass of water and cover loosely

with a plastic bag. It will keep for a week in the refrigerator. Or wash and dry it, and refrigerate in a small plastic bag with a dry paper towel inside to absorb any moisture.

Scallions

Scallions have a mild onion flavor. Store wrapped in plastic.

Equipment

Proper cooking equipment makes the work light and is a good cook's most prized possession. You can cook expertly without a store-bought steamer or even a food processor, but basic pans, knives, and a few other items are indispensable. Below are the things you need—and some attractive options—for preparing the menus in this volume.

Pots and pans

4- and 6-quart stockpots with covers
3 skillets (large, medium, small) with covers, one nonaluminum
Heavy-gauge sauté pan, 10 to 12 inches in diameter, with cover and ovenproof handle
3 saucepans with covers (1-, 2-, and 4-quart capacities)
  Choose heavy-gauge enameled cast-iron, plain cast-iron, aluminum-clad stainless steel, and aluminum (but you need at least one saucepan that is not aluminum). Best—but very expensive—is tin-lined copper.
Wok with cover
Steamer rack to fit wok or large saucepan
Roasting pan
15 x 10-inch baking pan
Two 17 x 11-inch baking sheets
9-inch square baking pan
9-inch pie pan
Large flameproof casserole with tight-fitting cover
Heatproof serving bowl or tureen
Heatproof serving platter
Four 6- to 8-ounce ramekins or small custard cups

Knives

A carbon-steel knife takes a sharp edge but tends to rust. You must wash and dry it after each use; otherwise it can blacken foods and counter tops. Good-quality stainless-steel knives, frequently honed, are less trouble and will serve just as well in the home kitchen. Never put a fine knife in the dishwasher. Rinse it, dry it, and put it away—but not loose in a drawer. Knives will stay sharp and last a long time if they have their own storage rack.
Small paring knife
10-inch chef's knife
Bread knife (serrated blade)
Sharpening steel

Other cooking tools

2 sets of mixing bowls in graduated sizes, one set preferably glass or stainless steel
Colander with a round base (stainless steel, aluminum, or enamel)
Large and small strainers in fine and coarse mesh
2 sieves in fine and coarse mesh
2 sets of measuring cups and spoons in graduated sizes
  One for dry ingredients, another for shortenings and liquids.
Cooking spoon
Slotted spoon
Long-handled wooden spoons
2 metal spatulas, or turners (for lifting hot foods from pans)
Rubber or vinyl spatula (for folding in ingredients)
Rolling pin
Grater (metal, with several sizes of holes)
  A rotary grater is handy for hard cheese.
2 wire whisks
Pair of metal tongs
Wooden board
Garlic press
Vegetable peeler
Mortar and pestle
Ladle
Pastry brush for basting (a small, new paintbrush that is not nylon serves well)
Stiff-bristled brush
Vegetable brush
Cooling rack
Kitchen scissors
Kitchen timer
Aluminum foil
Paper towels
Plastic wrap
Waxed paper
Brown paper bag
Thin rubber gloves

Electric appliances

Food processor or blender
  A blender will do most of the work required in this volume, but a food processor will do it more quickly and in larger volume. A food processor should be considered a necessity, not a luxury, for anyone who enjoys cooking.
Electric mixer

Optional cooking tools

Salad spinner
Flour sifter
Small jar with tight-fitting lid
Salad servers
Citrus juicer
  Inexpensive glass kind from the dime store will do.
Pastry blender
Zester
Roll of masking tape or white paper tape for labeling and dating

STOCKPOT

COLANDER

STRAINER

FOOD
PROCESSOR

RUBBER
SPATULA

WHISK

MIXING BOWLS

METAL
SPATULA

VEGETABLE PEELER

SHARPENING STEEL

CASSEROLE

CHEF'S KNIFE

PARING KNIFE

SAUCEPANS

TONGS

SAUTÉ PAN

SKILLET

Yvonne Gill

Trained as a cook by the French apprenticeship system—and having worked in the food field for 25 years—Yvonne Gill is an expert at preparing classic French recipes, which can take hours of cooking time. Here she updates some traditional soups and stews, modifying them to suit contemporary tastes and busy schedules.

In Menu 1, for instance, she offers an adaptation of a French *ragoût* (a thick stew of highly seasoned meat, poultry, or fish, and sometimes vegetables). In her version, made with veal, she thickens the stew by adding *crème fraîche* rather than flour. Watercress and endive are tossed with strips of Gruyère or Brebidor cheese for the salad.

Yvonne Gill showcases a Provençal favorite, the seafood soup known as *la bourride*, in Menu 2. Her recipe combines fish and shellfish in a wine-enriched stock flavored with leek, onion, fennel, and thyme. *Aïoli*, the French garlic mayonnaise, is stirred into the soup during the last minutes of cooking to give it a velvety texture and additional flavor.

For Menu 3, she creates a variation on *blanquette de veau* (a white veal stew finished with egg yolks and cream), using cubed chicken breast instead. To make this normally rich dish less caloric, she omits the egg yolks altogether. Young, tender green beans (called *haricots verts* in France) and tomatoes accompany the chicken, and a luscious raspberry tart concludes the meal.

Cubes of tender veal, pieces of red and yellow bell pepper, and whole pearl onions are the primary ingredients in this delicious ragoût. *A tossed salad of endive, watercress, and cheese accompanies the entrée.*

Veal Ragoût with Peppers
Autumn Salad

The sauce for this simple veal *ragoût* contains *crème fraîche*, a cultured cream product with a high butterfat content and a slightly tart, nutty taste. *Crème fraîche* is costly and not readily available except at specialty food stores and well-stocked supermarkets, so you can either substitute sour cream or make your own *crème fraîche* the day before you need it. Whisk 1 cup heavy cream into 1 cup sour cream or buttermilk at room temperature. Pour this mixture into a glass jar, cover it tightly, and let it stand in a warm place for 6 to 8 hours, then refrigerate. It will keep for up to 10 days.

Belgian endive, sold as compact heads that resemble plump cigars, is a slightly bitter member of the chicory family. Although it originated in Belgium, it is now being raised in this country as well. Belgian endive should be firm and very pale yellow to white. To keep it from discoloring, refrigerate it tightly wrapped in aluminum foil or waxed paper.

WHAT TO DRINK

This menu needs a wine with character, and the cook suggests a dry white from the Graves district of Bordeaux. Try a bottle from a small château.

SHOPPING LIST AND STAPLES

2 pounds veal round steak or veal blade roast, cut into 1-inch cubes
2 or 3 heads Belgian endive (about ¾ pound total weight)
Large bunch watercress
2 medium-size red bell peppers (about ½ pound total weight)
2 medium-size yellow bell peppers (about ½ pound total weight)
Small bunch fresh savory, or ½ teaspoon dried
Small bunch fresh marjoram, or ½ teaspoon dried
Small shallot
3 tablespoons crème fraîche, preferably homemade (see above), or commercial
2 tablespoons unsalted butter
¼ pound Gruyère or Brebidor cheese
10-ounce package frozen pearl onions
3 cups chicken stock, preferably homemade (see page 10), or canned
½ cup extra-virgin olive oil
2 teaspoons virgin olive oil

3 tablespoons raspberry vinegar
¼ cup all-purpose flour
1 bay leaf
Salt
Freshly ground pepper

UTENSILS

Large saucepan with cover
Small saucepan
Large heatproof dish
Large bowl
2 medium-size bowls
Salad spinner (optional)
Measuring cups and spoons
Chef's knife
Paring knife
Wooden spoon
Slotted spoon
Long-handled two-pronged fork
Whisk
Brown paper bag

START-TO-FINISH STEPS

1. Wash and dry fresh savory and marjoram, if using. Reserve 4 sprigs marjoram for garnish, if desired, and finely chop enough savory and remaining marjoram to measure 1 tablespoon each for veal recipe. Reserve remaining herbs for another use.
2. Follow salad recipe steps 1 and 2.
3. Follow veal recipe steps 1 through 6.
4. Follow salad recipe step 3.
5. Follow veal recipe steps 7 through 9.
6. Follow salad recipe steps 4 and 5.
7. Follow veal recipe steps 10 and 11 and serve with salad.

RECIPES

Veal Ragoût with Peppers

¼ cup all-purpose flour
⅛ teaspoon salt, approximately
⅛ teaspoon freshly ground pepper, approximately
2 pounds veal round steak or veal blade roast, cut into 1-inch cubes
3 cups chicken stock

2 tablespoons unsalted butter
2 teaspoons virgin olive oil
1 bay leaf
1 tablespoon finely chopped fresh savory, or ½ teaspoon
dried
1 tablespoon finely chopped fresh marjoram, plus 4 sprigs
for garnish (optional), or ½ teaspoon dried
2 medium-size red bell peppers (about ½ pound total
weight)
2 medium-size yellow bell peppers (about ½ pound total
weight)
10-ounce package frozen pearl onions
3 tablespoons crème fraîche, preferably homemade (see
page 18), or commercial

1. Combine flour, ⅛ teaspoon salt, and ⅛ teaspoon pepper
on sheet of waxed paper. Dredge veal in seasoned flour,
shaking off excess, and set veal aside.
2. In small saucepan, heat chicken stock over medium-
high heat until hot.
3. Meanwhile, in large saucepan, heat 1 tablespoon butter
and 1 teaspoon oil over medium-high heat just until butter
foams. Add half the veal and cook 3 to 4 minutes, stirring
occasionally, until lightly browned on all sides. Using
slotted spoon, transfer veal to medium-size bowl. Add
remaining butter and oil to pan and cook remaining veal in
same manner.
4. Return veal in bowl to pan and pour in ½ cup hot stock.
Increase heat to high and bring stock to a boil. Boil rapidly
1 minute, scraping up brown bits clinging to bottom of pan.
5. Pour remaining hot stock over veal and add bay leaf,
savory, and chopped marjoram. Reduce heat to low and
simmer veal, partially covered, 20 to 30 minutes, or until
nearly tender.
6. Meanwhile, roast peppers: One by one, pierce peppers
through top with long-handled two-pronged fork and hold
directly over gas flame, turning to char skins evenly. Or,
place on broiler rack set 3 inches from heating element and
broil, turning peppers to char skins evenly. Transfer peppers to brown paper bag, close bag, and set peppers aside
to steam. Preheat oven to 200 degrees.
7. When peppers are cool enough to handle, hold under
cold running water and rub gently to remove skins. Halve,
core, and seed peppers; cut into 1½-inch squares.
8. When veal is nearly tender, add peppers and onions to
saucepan and simmer 5 minutes, or until onions are
thawed.

9. Using slotted spoon, transfer veal, peppers, and onions
to large heatproof dish and keep warm in oven.
10. Increase heat under saucepan to high and boil liquid
remaining in pan 3 to 4 minutes, or until reduced to 2 cups.
Reduce heat to medium and whisk in crème fraîche. Season with salt and pepper, if desired.
11. Remove veal, peppers, and onions from oven, return
to sauce, and stir well. Divide ragoût among 4 dinner
plates and garnish each plate with a sprig of marjoram, if
desired.

Autumn Salad

2 to 3 heads Belgian endive (about ¾ pound total weight)
Large bunch watercress
Small shallot
¼ pound Gruyère or Brebidor cheese
3 tablespoons raspberry vinegar
½ cup extra-virgin olive oil
Freshly ground pepper

1. Wash endive and watercress and dry in salad spinner or
with paper towels. Trim endive and separate into leaves.
Trim and discard tough ends from watercress, leaving
stems whole. Place endive and watercress in plastic bag
and chill 30 minutes. Peel and mince enough shallot to
measure 1 teaspoon; set aside.
2. Cut cheese into 2-inch-long by ¼-inch-wide strips.
3. For dressing, combine minced shallot, vinegar, and ¼
cup oil in medium-size bowl. Whisking constantly, add
remaining ¼ cup oil in a slow steady stream and continue
whisking until well blended. Add pepper to taste.
4. Remove endive and watercress from refrigerator. Place
4 or 5 endive leaves together and cut diagonally into 4
pieces; proceed in same manner for remaining endive.
5. In large bowl, combine endive, watercress, and cheese.
Stir dressing to recombine, if necessary. Drizzle dressing
over salad and toss lightly until evenly coated. Divide
salad equally among 4 small plates.

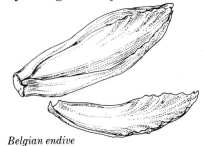

Belgian endive

Bourride with Aïoli

Bright pottery soup bowls show off the bourride, *a garlic-flavored fish soup popular in Provence. This version has a colorful garnish of lemon and orange peel, red bell pepper, and a sprig of lemon thyme. Serve it with French bread.*

For this satisfying soup-stew, you can vary the fish according to availability, but those with firm flesh have the best texture and flavor. You will also need 2½ pounds of fish bones, heads, and tails, so ask your fish dealer to give you the trimmings from the fish you order.

Lemon thyme, which is less strong and more tangy than other varieties of thyme, is the predominant seasoning in the stew. If it is not available, use another variety of fresh thyme, but decrease the amount used from 1 tablespoon to 1 teaspoon.

WHAT TO DRINK

A full-bodied white wine is highly recommended here. A white Châteauneuf-du-Pape would be excellent, as would an Italian Greco di Tufo or a white Spanish Rioja.

SHOPPING LIST AND STAPLES

1 pound blackfish (grouper) or red snapper fillets
½ pound cod or haddock fillets
½ pound sea bass or bluefish fillets
16 to 20 mussels, cleaned, with beards removed
2½ pounds fish bones, heads, and tails
Medium-size red bell pepper
Medium-size tomato
2 fennel bulbs (about 1½ pounds total weight)
Medium-size leek
Medium-size onion
4 large cloves garlic
Small bunch fresh lemon thyme or other fresh thyme,
    or ½ teaspoon dried
Small orange
2 lemons
8 eggs
2 cups good-quality olive oil, approximately
1 long loaf French bread
2 bay leaves
10 white peppercorns
Salt and freshly ground pepper
1 cup dry white wine

UTENSILS

Food processor or blender
Electric mixer

Large heavy-gauge stockpot
2-quart stockpot with cover
Large saucepan
Small saucepan
Large shallow heatproof dish
Large bowl
3-quart nonaluminum bowl
2 small bowls
Large strainer
Measuring cups and spoons
Chef's knife
Paring knife
Slotted spoon
Ladle
Whisk
Cheesecloth
Garlic press

START-TO-FINISH STEPS

1. Wash lemons and orange and dry with paper towels. Using vegetable peeler or sharp paring knife, remove eight 3-inch-long by ¼-inch-wide strips of rind from orange and lemons for bourride recipe. Squeeze enough lemon juice to measure 3 tablespoons for aïoli recipe. Separate 8 eggs, placing 4 yolks in small bowl for bourride recipe and 4 yolks in another small bowl for aïoli recipe. Reserve whites for another use.
2. Follow bourride recipe steps 1 through 7.
3. Follow aïoli recipe steps 1 through 3.
4. Follow bourride recipe steps 8 through 13 and serve.

RECIPES

Bourride with Aïoli

Medium-size leek
2 fennel bulbs (about 1½ pounds total weight)
Medium-size onion
Medium-size red bell pepper
Small bunch fresh lemon thyme or other fresh thyme, or
   ½ teaspoon dried
1 pound blackfish (grouper) or red snapper fillets
½ pound cod or haddock fillets
½ pound sea bass or bluefish fillets
2½ pounds fish bones, heads, and tails
7 tablespoons good-quality olive oil

Medium-size tomato
1 cup dry white wine
2 bay leaves
10 white peppercorns
Eight 3-inch-long by ¼-inch-wide strips lemon rind
Eight 3-inch-long by ¼-inch-wide strips orange rind
Salt and freshly ground pepper
16 to 20 mussels, cleaned, with beards removed
4 egg yolks
1 cup Aïoli (see following recipe)
1 long loaf French bread

1. Trim off root end of leek and split leek lengthwise. Separate leaves and rinse well to remove any sand and grit. Dry with paper towel. Cut white part of leek crosswise into ⅛-inch-thick slices and green part into ¼-inch-thick slices. You should have about ½ cup each.
2. Trim stalks and root end from fennel and discard. Halve fennel bulbs and rinse under cold running water. Dry with paper towels and chop finely. Peel onion and chop finely.
3. Wash and dry bell pepper, and fresh thyme if using. Halve, core, and seed pepper. Cut one half of pepper into 8 strips and reserve remaining half for another use. Reserve 4 sprigs thyme for garnish and mince enough remaining thyme to measure 1 tablespoon if using lemon thyme, or 1 teaspoon if using other type of fresh thyme.
4. Cut fish fillets into 1½-inch chunks. Cut fish bones into 6-inch pieces. Leave heads and tails intact. Bring 2 cups water to a boil in small saucepan over high heat.
5. Meanwhile, heat 4 tablespoons olive oil in large heavy-gauge stockpot over medium heat until hot. Add green part of leek, fennel, and onion, and cook, stirring occasionally, 5 minutes, or until vegetables are soft.
6. While vegetables are cooking, blanch tomato in small saucepan of boiling water 30 seconds; remove with slotted spoon. Core, peel, and halve tomato. Squeeze out seeds and chop tomato finely; set aside.
7. Add fish bones, heads, and tails to vegetables in stockpot, increase heat to medium high, and cook 2 to 3 minutes, or until vegetables turn opaque. Add wine and boil over high heat 1 minute. Add 7 cups water, minced fresh thyme or dried thyme, bay leaves, peppercorns, 2 strips lemon rind, and 2 strips orange rind. Reduce heat to low and simmer stock, uncovered, 25 minutes.
8. Strain stock through large strainer lined with double layer of cheesecloth and set over large bowl. There should be about 7 cups stock. Discard solids left in strainer. Rinse out stockpot.

9. In same stockpot, heat remaining 3 tablespoons olive oil over medium heat until hot. Add white part of leek and chopped tomato, and cook 1 minute. Add strained stock and bring to a simmer. Add salt and pepper to taste, and another 2 strips each of lemon and orange rind. Simmer stock 5 minutes. Preheat oven to 200 degrees.

10. Meanwhile, ladle ½ cup simmering stock into 2-quart stockpot. Add mussels and cook over high heat, covered tightly, 1 to 2 minutes, or until mussels open. Turn off heat and discard any unopened mussels.

11. Add fish pieces to *large* stockpot in single layer and poach, covered, 2 to 3 minutes, or until fish is just cooked through. Using slotted spoon, transfer fish in single layer to large shallow heatproof dish and cover with 1 cup stock. Add mussels to dish and cover with waxed paper. Place dish in oven to keep warm.

12. Using electric mixer, beat egg yolks in small bowl 1 minute, or until lemon yellow. Bring 2 inches water to a simmer in large saucepan. Place 3-quart nonaluminum bowl over saucepan, being careful not to let bottom of bowl touch water. Place 1 cup aïoli in bowl and add beaten egg yolks. Whisk mixture 1 minute, or until warm to touch. Add remaining 5½ cups stock and cook, whisking constantly, 1 minute, or until it is the consistency of a very thin custard. Remove bowl from pan immediately to prevent curdling.

13. Remove seafood from oven and divide among 4 soup bowls. Ladle in soup and garnish each serving with 2 pepper strips, a strip of lemon and orange rind, and a sprig of fresh thyme. Serve bourride with slices of French bread and remaining aïoli on the side.

Aïoli

4 egg yolks
4 large cloves garlic
1½ cups good-quality olive oil
3 tablespoons lemon juice
Freshly ground pepper

1. Place egg yolks in food processor or blender and process until very thick and lemon yellow in color.

2. Crush and peel garlic and force cloves through garlic press directly into processor or blender. Process until combined.

3. With machine running, add oil in a slow steady stream. With machine still running, gradually add lemon juice. Season with pepper to taste. Transfer aïoli to small bowl.

▬▬▬▬▬▬
ADDED TOUCH
Pouring the dressing over the potatoes while they are still warm gives this recipe added flavor. If you must prepare this recipe ahead of time, be sure to bring the salad to room temperature before serving.

Country Salad

Small bunch parsley
Small bunch tarragon
2 pounds small new potatoes
Small grapefruit
Small fennel bulb (about ½ pound)
Medium-size shallot
⅓ cup good-quality olive oil, preferably extra-virgin
Salt and freshly ground pepper
2 tablespoons dry white wine, approximately

1. Wash herbs and potatoes and dry with paper towels. Mince enough parsley to measure 1 tablespoon. Reserve 4 sprigs tarragon for garnish and coarsely chop enough remaining tarragon to measure 1 teaspoon. Reserve remaining herbs for another use. Squeeze enough grapefruit juice to measure ¼ cup.

2. Trim stalks and root end from fennel and discard. Wash fennel bulb under cold running water and dry with paper towels. Cut fennel bulb into ⅛-inch-thick strips. Peel and mince shallot.

3. Fit medium-size saucepan with vegetable steamer and fill pan with enough water to come up to but not above bottom of steamer. Bring water to a boil over medium-high heat.

4. Place potatoes in steamer, cover pan, and steam 25 to 30 minutes, or until potatoes are just tender.

5. In medium-size bowl, combine grapefruit juice, shallot, and 2 tablespoons olive oil and whisk until combined. Whisking constantly, add remaining oil in a slow, steady stream.

6. While potatoes are still hot, peel them and cut each potato into 3 slices. Place slices in single layer in shallow dish. Season with salt and pepper to taste and drizzle with wine. (Use only as much wine as potatoes will absorb. There should be no excess wine in dish.)

7. Sprinkle potatoes with herbs and add strips of fennel. Pour dressing over potatoes and fennel and fold together lightly but thoroughly.

8. Divide salad among 4 small plates and garnish each plate with a tarragon sprig.

Blanquette of Chicken with Morels
Baby Green Bean and Tomato Salad
Raspberry Tart

For an elegant dinner, offer guests a blanquette *of chicken, green beans and tomatoes, and a raspberry tart for dessert.*

The chicken dish calls for unusual, meaty-tasting morel mushrooms. Available fresh or dried, morels are dark brown to off-white with conical pitted caps. Fresh morels are moist and often quite dirty; be sure to rinse them thoroughly before using. If you must store fresh morels, spread them in a single layer in a dish in the refrigerator. If damp, cover them with a paper towel; if dry, cover them with a piece of barely moistened cheesecloth and use them within three days. Dried morels must be soaked in warm water until they are soft enough to be cut. Cook them as you would fresh, but use a lesser amount because they have a much stronger flavor.

To give the *blanquette* a different taste altogether, you can substitute fresh or dried chanterelles. These trumpet-shaped mushrooms are apricot-gold in color and have a flavor that is sometimes described as softly spicy. Dried chanterelles should be soaked for at least half an hour before cooking.

Fresh morels are available in specialty food shops from early spring into summer; fresh chanterelles may be purchased during the fall and winter.

WHAT TO DRINK

A firm and fruity white wine would match these dishes well. Choose a French Sancerre or Pouilly-Fumé, a California Sauvignon Blanc, or an Italian Pinot Blanc.

SHOPPING LIST AND STAPLES

2 whole skinless, boneless chicken breasts (about 2 pounds total weight)
6 ounces fresh morels, or 2 ounces dried
1 pound haricots verts, or other young green beans
2 medium-size tomatoes (about 1 pound total weight)
Large shallot
Small bunch fresh rosemary, or ½ teaspoon dried
1½ pints fresh raspberries, or two 12-ounce bags frozen unsweetened
3 eggs
1 pint heavy cream
4 tablespoons unsalted butter
1-pound package frozen puff pastry

23

2½ cups chicken stock, preferably homemade (see page 10), or canned
¼ cup walnut oil
2 tablespoons good-quality olive oil
3 tablespoons basil or other good quality herb vinegar
1 tablespoon all-purpose flour
4 tablespoons granulated sugar
2 tablespoons confectioners' sugar
Salt and freshly ground pepper

UTENSILS

6-quart stockpot
4-quart stockpot
Large sauté pan with cover
2 large saucepans
Baking sheet
9-inch tart pan with removable bottom
Large nonaluminum bowl
5 small bowls
Colander
Small strainer
Measuring cups and spoons
Chef's knife
Paring knife
Slotted spoon
Whisk
Pastry brush
Rolling pin
Paper doily (optional)

START-TO-FINISH STEPS

One hour ahead: Set out puff pastry, and frozen raspberries if using, to thaw for tart recipe. If using dried morels, combine with 3 cups warm water in small bowl and let soak for blanquette recipe.

1. Follow blanquette recipe steps 1 through 4.
2. Follow tart recipe steps 1 through 3.
3. Follow blanquette recipe step 5.
4. While chicken poaches, follow tart recipe steps 4 through 8.
5. While tart bakes, follow blanquette recipe steps 6 and 7 and salad recipe steps 1 and 2.
6. Follow blanquette recipe step 8 and tart recipe steps 9 and 10.
7. While tart finishes baking, follow salad recipe steps 3 through 6.
8. Follow blanquette recipe steps 9 through 11 and tart recipe step 11. Serve blanquette with salad.
9. Follow tart recipe step 12 and serve for dessert.

RECIPES

Blanquette of Chicken with Morels

6 ounces fresh morels, or 2 ounces dried, soaked
Small bunch fresh rosemary, or ½ teaspoon dried

4 tablespoons unsalted butter
1 tablespoon all-purpose flour
2 whole skinless, boneless chicken breasts (about 2 pounds total weight)
2½ cups chicken stock
Salt and freshly ground pepper
½ cup heavy cream

1. In 6-quart stockpot, bring 2 quarts water to a boil over high heat.
2. Meanwhile, if using fresh morels, rinse and set aside. Wash and dry fresh rosemary, if using. Set aside 6 sprigs rosemary; reserve remainder for another use.
3. Knead together 2 tablespoons butter and 1 tablespoon flour and set aside.
4. Cut chicken into 1-inch pieces. Add chicken to boiling water and cook 1 minute, or until it turns opaque and feels firm to the touch. Turn chicken into colander to drain.
5. In 4-quart stockpot, combine stock and 1 sprig fresh rosemary or ½ teaspoon dried. Bring stock to a boil over medium-high heat and simmer 5 minutes. Add chicken, and season with salt and pepper to taste. Reduce heat to very low and poach chicken, uncovered, at a bare simmer, 10 minutes, or until just tender.
6. Drain dried morels, if using, and pat dry with paper towels. Heat remaining 2 tablespoons butter in large sauté pan over medium heat until butter foams. Add fresh or dried morels to pan and toss to coat. Reduce heat to medium-low and cook, covered, 2 minutes. Remove cover, increase heat to medium, and sauté, tossing frequently, another minute. Season with salt and pepper to taste.
7. Add morels and cooking liquid to chicken and cook at a bare simmer 5 minutes.
8. Using slotted spoon, transfer chicken and morels to large saucepan and set aside. Increase heat to medium-high and boil poaching liquid 7 to 8 minutes, or until reduced to 2¼ cups.
9. Add heavy cream and whisk until combined. Reduce heat to medium and whisk in butter and flour mixture, a bit at a time. Simmer 1 minute.
10. Pour sauce over chicken and morels and stir to coat evenly. Cook over very low heat 1 minute, or until chicken and morels are heated through.
11. Transfer blanquette to large serving bowl and garnish with remaining rosemary sprigs.

Baby Green Bean and Tomato Salad

Salt
1 pound haricots verts, or other young green beans
2 medium-size tomatoes (about 1 pound total weight)
Large shallot
¼ cup walnut oil
3 tablespoons basil or other good-quality herb vinegar
2 tablespoons good-quality olive oil
Salt and freshly ground pepper

1. Bring 2 quarts water and 2 teaspoons salt to a boil in large saucepan.

2. Meanwhile, trim and discard stem ends of beans. Place beans in colander and rinse under cold running water; set aside. Wash tomatoes and dry with paper towels. Core tomatoes and cut into wedges. Peel and mince shallot.

3. For dressing, in small bowl, combine shallot, 2 tablespoons walnut oil, and vinegar, and whisk until blended. Whisking constantly, add remaining 2 tablespoons walnut oil and olive oil in a slow steady stream. Season with salt and pepper to taste.

4. Add beans to boiling water and blanch 30 seconds. Turn beans into colander, refresh briefly under cold running water, and drain thoroughly.

5. Turn beans into large nonaluminum bowl, add half of dressing, and toss until evenly coated.

6. Transfer beans to large serving platter, arrange tomato wedges around beans, and drizzle remaining dressing over tomatoes.

Raspberry Tart

3 eggs
1½ pints fresh raspberries, or two 12-ounce bags frozen unsweetened, thawed
1-pound package frozen puff pastry, thawed
2 to 4 tablespoons granulated sugar
½ cup heavy cream
2 tablespoons confectioners' sugar

1. Preheat oven to 400 degrees.

2. Separate eggs, placing yolks in small bowl and reserving whites for another use. For glaze, whisk together 1 egg yolk and 2 tablespoons water in small bowl.

3. If using fresh raspberries, gently rinse under cold running water. Transfer to double thickness of paper towels and pat dry.

4. Roll out half of puff pastry to ¼-inch thickness on lightly floured surface. Place in 9-inch tart pan set on baking sheet. Prick bottom of pastry with fork and trim pastry to edge of pan.

5. Fill pastry shell with raspberries and sprinkle with granulated sugar to taste, depending on tartness of berries.

6. On lightly floured surface, roll out remaining puff pastry into 9½-inch circle. Using rim of small glass, cut a hole in center of circle.

7. Brush outside edge of filled pastry shell with egg glaze. Drape pastry circle over pastry shell and press lightly around edges to seal. Trim excess dough and discard.

8. Brush top of tart with egg glaze and bake in center of oven 20 minutes, or until pastry is puffed and lightly browned.

9. Whisk together remaining 2 egg yolks and cream in small bowl. Pull oven rack toward you and pour custard through center hole in pastry. (Pour slowly so custard has time to filter through fruit.)

10. Reduce oven temperature to 350 degrees and bake tart an additional 15 minutes to set custard.

11. Remove tart from oven and allow to cool at least 10 minutes.

12. Just before serving, place confectioners' sugar in small strainer. Lay paper doily over tart and sift sugar over it to form decorative pattern. Or, sift sugar directly onto tart. Serve tart directly from pan or remove tart from pan and serve on platter.

ADDED TOUCH

You can serve this classic French soup hot or cold instead of the *blanquette*. If you prefer it cold, sieve the ingredients, add the cream, then chill the mixture thoroughly. Do not use a food processor or blender or the soup will lose body and texture. This recipe yields about 13 cups. If desired, reduce the ingredients by half, or follow the recipe up to step 8 and freeze half the soup for later use.

Potato and Leek Soup

2 pounds Idaho potatoes
1 stalk celery
Small sprig marjoram
Small bunch chives
Medium-size onion
Large leek (about ¾ pound)
6 white peppercorns
8 cups chicken stock
4 tablespoons unsalted butter
2 bay leaves
Salt
1 cup heavy cream
½ cup crème fraîche, preferably homemade (see page 18), or commercial (optional)

1. Wash potatoes, celery, marjoram, and chives and dry with paper towels. Peel potatoes and cut into ½-inch dice. Trim celery and cut into ¼-inch dice. Mince marjoram. Snip enough chives to measure 3 tablespoons.

2. Peel onion and cut into ¼-inch dice. Trim leek and split lengthwise. Separate leaves and rinse thoroughly to remove any sand and grit. Pat leek dry with paper towel and cut crosswise into ¼-inch-thick slices. Crush peppercorns under flat blade of chef's knife.

3. Place potatoes in colander and rinse briefly under cold running water to remove starch. Dry with paper towels.

4. In small saucepan, heat stock over medium-high heat until hot.

5. Heat butter in large stockpot over medium-low heat until it foams. Add onion, celery, and leek. Cook vegetables, covered, 5 minutes, or until softened. Add potatoes and cook, covered, 5 minutes.

6. Add crushed peppercorns, marjoram, bay leaves, hot stock, and salt to taste. Simmer 20 to 25 minutes, or until potatoes are tender but not mushy.

7. Force soup through fine sieve or food mill into large bowl. Discard solids remaining in strainer.

8. Transfer soup to stockpot. Over low heat, add cream, and heat, stirring, until hot.

9. Ladle soup into individual bowls and garnish each serving with chives, and crème fraîche if desired.

Jerry Di Vecchio

MENU 1 (Right)
Crisp Pork with Peanut Sauce and
Cellophane Noodles
Stir-fried Bok Choy
Steamed Ginger Custards

MENU 2
Scallop Ball Soup with Shrimp and
Mustard Greens
Coriander-Shallot Chopstick Rolls
Pineapple with Lime, Mint, and
Red Pepper Flakes

MENU 3
Mock Mascarpone with Watercress
Mongolian Lamb and Vegetable Soup
Szechwan Pepper Buttons

Because she has spent most of her life on the West
Coast, Jerry Di Vecchio is an ardent admirer of
what is currently known as "California cuisine,"
a style of cooking that stresses the innovative
use of fresh ingredients. But her love of fine foods has
never been limited to what she finds in her home state.
Influenced by her world travels, she often creates menus
that blend the disciplines and flavors of several cuisines.

In Menu 1, the focus is an Indonesian-style stew of roast
pork served on a bed of soft cellophane noodles. Unlike
Western stews, the meat and sauce (a sweetened peanut
butter mixture) are not combined until serving time. The
cook recommends using a wok, an indispensable tool in
Oriental cooking, to stir fry the side dish of *bok choy* and to
steam the gingery egg custards for dessert.

In true Thai fashion, the scallop ball soup with shrimp
and mustard greens of Menu 2 is seasoned with ginger,
lime juice, and pepper to create a dish that is at once
piquant and subtle, sharp and sweet. Unusual chopstick
rolls (egg-roll wrappers baked with a filling of coriander
and shallots) are a crisp accompaniment to the soup.

Jerry Di Vecchio combines an assortment of baked vegetables with strips of stir-fried lamb in a clear broth ac-
cented with sherry for the main-course soup of Menu 3.
The meal begins with mock *mascarpone* served in individual ramekins and ends with buttery cookies sparked with
Szechwan peppercorns.

*Indonesian-style pork stew with peanut sauce nestled on a
bed of cellophane noodles and garnished with frilly scallion
brushes is an exotic meal guaranteed to impress company.
Garlic-flavored* bok choy *is the side dish, and steamed ginger
custards end the meal.*

Crisp Pork with Peanut Sauce and Cellophane Noodles
Stir-fried Bok Choy
Steamed Ginger Custards

The exotic pork stew is served with cellophane noodles, slender translucent strands made from ground mung beans. Also known as bean threads, or *saifun*, these noodles require soaking in hot tap water. Do not remove the rubber band or string before soaking the bean threads or they will become too unmanageable to cut. Just before draining, snip the rubber band or string and discard it. Cellophane noodles are sold in any Oriental market or in a well-stocked supermarket with an Oriental foods section.

Bok choy, a variety of Chinese cabbage, is a versatile Oriental vegetable with thick, rounded white stalks and broad green leaves. Its taste is vaguely reminiscent of Swiss chard. If you cannot find it, use broccoli instead.

WHAT TO DRINK

A spicy white wine, perhaps with a touch of sweetness, would be appropriate with this menu. A German Riesling is a good choice. Alternatively, select a Chinese or Japanese beer, or fruit juice.

SHOPPING LIST AND STAPLES

1½ pounds well-larded boned pork shoulder, cut into ½-inch cubes
Medium-size head bok choy (about 1¾ pounds)
Small bunch scallions
3 medium-size cloves garlic
3 large eggs
1 pint light cream
1½ cups chicken stock, preferably homemade (see page 10), or canned
6-ounce jar creamy peanut butter
4 tablespoons soy sauce, approximately
2 tablespoons rice vinegar
2 tablespoons vegetable oil
4-ounce package cellophane noodles (bean threads or saifun)
2 tablespoons plus 2 teaspoons sugar
1 teaspoon red pepper flakes, approximately
3-ounce box crystallized ginger
2 tablespoons dry sherry

UTENSILS

Wok with cover (optional)
Large heavy-gauge skillet (if not using wok)
Large saucepan with cover (if not using wok)
2 small saucepans
Steamer rack to fit wok or large saucepan
15 x 10-inch baking pan
Medium-size bowl
2 small bowls
2 strainers, coarse and fine mesh
Measuring cups and spoons
Chef's knife
Paring knife
2 wooden spoons
Whisk
Metal spatula
Four 6-ounce Oriental teacups or custard cups

START-TO-FINISH STEPS

One hour ahead: Set out eggs to come to room temperature for custards recipe.

1. Peel garlic and mince 2 cloves for pork recipe and 1 clove for bok choy recipe; set aside.
2. Follow pork recipe step 1 and bok choy recipe step 1.
3. Follow pork recipe steps 2 and 3 and custards recipe steps 1 through 5.
4. Follow pork recipe step 4 and custards recipe step 6.
5. Follow pork recipe steps 5 through 9.
6. Follow bok choy recipe steps 2 and 3.
7. Follow pork recipe step 10 and serve with bok choy.
8. Follow custards recipe step 7 and serve for dessert.

RECIPES

Crisp Pork with Peanut Sauce and Cellophane Noodles

1½ pounds well-larded boned pork shoulder, cut into ½-inch cubes
2 medium-size cloves garlic, minced
½ to 1 teaspoon red pepper flakes
4 scallions
1½ cups chicken stock
4-ounce package cellophane noodles (bean threads or saifun)
½ cup creamy peanut butter
2 tablespoons soy sauce
2 tablespoons rice vinegar

2 tablespoons dry sherry
2 teaspoons sugar

1. Preheat oven to 475 degrees.
2. Combine pork, garlic, and red pepper flakes in 15 x 10-inch baking pan and mix well. Bake pork, stirring often with metal spatula, about 25 minutes, or until sizzling.
3. Meanwhile, prepare scallion brushes. Wash, dry, and trim scallions, leaving about 2 inches of green tops. With tip of paring knife, slice thinly down about 1 inch all around bulb. Fill small bowl with cold water and immerse scallions. Ends will curl in water. (See illustrations below.) Place in refrigerator until ready to serve.

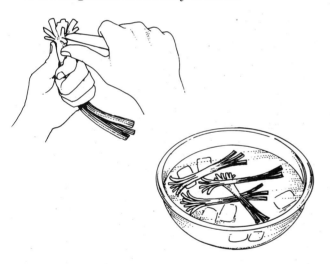

4. When pork is cooked, add 1¼ cups stock to pan; stir well and cover pan with foil. Turn off oven and keep pork warm in oven with door ajar until needed.
5. Fill medium-size bowl with hot tap water. Add cellophane noodles and allow to soak 5 minutes.
6. Meanwhile, combine peanut butter and soy sauce in small saucepan and stir until smooth. Gradually add vinegar, sherry, remaining ¼ cup stock, and sugar. (If liquid is added too quickly, peanut butter may not readily blend with it.) Set aside.
7. Bring 3 cups water to a boil in small saucepan.
8. Drain cellophane noodles in strainer. Add to boiling water and cook 2 to 3 minutes, or until just translucent. Turn noodles into strainer, shake to remove excess water, and transfer to serving platter.
9. Cook peanut sauce over medium-high heat, stirring constantly, until bubbling, about 2 minutes. Remove pan from heat at once.

10. Spoon pork over noodles and top with peanut sauce. Garnish with scallion brushes. ·

Stir-fried Bok Choy

Medium-size head bok choy (about 1¾ pounds)
2 tablespoons vegetable oil
1 medium-size clove garlic, minced
1 to 2 tablespoons soy sauce, approximately

1. Cut off stem end from bok choy and separate stalks. Wash and dry with paper towels. Trim off white part of each stalk and cut white parts diagonally into 1-inch pieces. Cut green leaves into 1-inch-wide strips.
2. In wok or large heavy-gauge skillet, heat vegetable oil over high heat until hot. Add garlic and white parts of bok choy and stir fry 2 minutes. Add 2 tablespoons water and stir fry another 1 to 2 minutes.
3. Add bok choy leaves and 1 tablespoon water and stir fry 30 seconds, or until leaves are wilted. Season with soy sauce to taste, toss gently, and transfer to serving platter.

Steamed Ginger Custards

3-ounce box crystallized ginger
1½ cups light cream
3 large eggs, at room temperature
2 tablespoons sugar

1. Using chef's knife, cut enough ginger into small pieces to measure 3 tablespoons.
2. Combine cream, eggs, and sugar in small bowl and whisk just until blended.
3. Pour egg mixture through fine strainer into four 6-ounce Oriental teacups or custard cups. Add 1½ teaspoons ginger to each cup.
4. Cover cups tightly with foil. Place steamer rack in wok or large saucepan containing about 2 inches of water (when water boils it should not touch rack). Bring water to a boil over high heat.
5. Set cups on rack, cover wok or pan, and reduce heat to medium-low. Steam custards over gently boiling water 20 to 25 minutes, or until they appear almost set when shaken gently (remove foil to check).
6. Remove custards from wok or pan and set aside to cool. Custards will look soft in center but will continue to cook when removed from heat.
7. Just before serving, garnish each custard with a few remaining pieces of ginger.

Scallop Ball Soup with Shrimp and Mustard Greens
Coriander-Shallot Chopstick Rolls
Pineapple with Lime, Mint, and Red Pepper Flakes

A Thai soup with shrimp, mustard greens, and scallop balls goes well with chopstick rolls and a piquant pineapple dessert.

The delicate scallop dumplings are an easier-to-handle variation of French *quenelles*. The tender balls firm up quickly during poaching and can be held, if necessary, before reheating. If you cannot purchase mustard greens, use watercress in the soup.

The cook uses Chinese egg-roll wrappers, or skins, for the "chopstick" rolls, which are delicious eaten alone or dipped into the soup. Egg-roll wrappers are pastry squares measuring from 5 to 8 inches. They are sold in one-pound packages (about 24 skins to a pound) in the refrigerator sections of Chinese markets and many well-stocked supermarkets. Coriander, also known as cilantro or Chinese parsley, is combined with shallots in the filling for the rolls. Coriander resembles flat-leaf parsley but its leaves are paler green. Fresh coriander has a very pungent aroma and flavor, so gauge the amount to your taste.

WHAT TO DRINK
The cook suggests serving a dry white Spanish Gran Viña Sol or a California Folle Blanche.

SHOPPING LIST AND STAPLES
½ pound medium-size shrimp
½ pound bay scallops
½ pound mustard greens
Large bunch scallions
3 medium-size shallots
1-inch piece fresh ginger
Large bunch coriander
Small bunch mint
Medium-size pineapple (3 to 3½ pounds)
3 large limes
Medium-size lemon
1 egg
3 tablespoons unsalted butter
1-pound package egg-roll wrappers
6⅓ cups chicken stock, preferably homemade (see page 10), or canned
12-ounce bottle Oriental fish sauce, or ¼ cup soy sauce (optional)
2 tablespoons sugar
½ teaspoon red pepper flakes, approximately
Salt
Freshly ground white pepper

UTENSILS
Food processor or blender
Small skillet
Large saucepan with cover
2 small saucepans, 1 nonaluminum
9-inch square baking pan
Large platter
Medium-size bowl

Small bowl
Measuring cups and spoons
Chef's knife
Paring knife
2 wooden spoons
Slotted spoon
Ladle
Citrus juicer (optional)
Vegetable peeler (optional)
Pastry brush
Zester or grater

START-TO-FINISH STEPS
1. Wash and dry coriander, limes, and lemon. Coarsely chop enough coriander to measure ¼ cup for soup recipe and ½ to 1 cup for chopstick rolls recipe. Using zester or grater, remove enough zest from 1 lime to measure 2 tablespoons and cut 4 thin slices from center of second lime for pineapple recipe. Squeeze enough juice from remaining portions of same 2 limes to measure 3 tablespoons for pineapple recipe. Quarter third lime for soup recipe. Using vegetable peeler or paring knife, cut 3-inch strip of lemon rind; halve lemon and squeeze enough juice to measure 2 tablespoons for soup recipe. Set aside.
2. Follow soup recipe steps 1 through 3, chopstick rolls recipe steps 1 and 2, and pineapple recipe step 1.
3. Follow soup recipe steps 4 through 7.
4. Follow chopstick rolls recipe steps 3 through 6.
5. While chopstick rolls are baking, follow pineapple recipe steps 2 and 3 and soup recipe step 8.
6. Follow chopstick rolls recipe step 7, soup recipe step 9, and pineapple recipe step 4.
7. Follow soup recipe step 10 and serve with chopstick rolls.
8. Follow pineapple recipe step 5 and serve for dessert.

RECIPES

Scallop Ball Soup with Shrimp and Mustard Greens
½ pound medium-size shrimp
½ pound bay scallops
1-inch piece fresh ginger
1 egg
½ pound mustard greens
7 scallions
6⅓ cups chicken stock
Salt
Freshly ground white pepper
3-inch strip lemon rind
2 tablespoons lemon juice
¼ cup coarsely chopped coriander
¼ cup Oriental fish sauce or soy sauce (optional)
1 lime, quartered

1. Pinch off legs of shrimp, several at a time, then bend back and snap off sharp, beaklike pieces of shell just above

31

tail. Remove and discard shell. Using sharp paring knife, make shallow incision along back of each shrimp, exposing black digestive vein. Extract vein and discard.

2. Rinse scallops and dry with paper towels; set aside. Cut two ¼-inch-thick slices of ginger; mince enough remaining ginger to measure ½ teaspoon; set aside.

Fresh ginger

3. Separate egg, dropping white into small bowl and reserving yolk for another use. Wash mustard greens and scallions and dry with paper towels. Trim stems from mustard greens and cut leaves into 1-inch-wide strips. Trim scallions and cut on diagonal into thin slices; set aside.

4. Place 1 ginger slice and 3 cups water in small saucepan and bring water to a boil over high heat.

5. Meanwhile, in food processor or blender, combine minced ginger, scallops, egg white, and ⅓ cup stock. Process 1 minute, or until mixture is smooth. Season with salt and pepper to taste. Line platter with double thickness of paper towels.

6. When water boils, reduce heat to keep water at a bare simmer. To shape scallop balls, immerse 2 tablespoons in a glass of cold water. With one wet spoon, scoop up a heaping tablespoonful of scallop mixture. Smooth ball with back of second wet spoon and gently nudge it off into the simmering water. Working quickly, repeat for remaining scallop mixture, rewetting spoons for each ball. You should have 10 to 12 balls. Adjust heat, if necessary, to keep water at the very low simmer. Poach scallop balls 3 to 5 minutes, or until they turn white and float on the surface of the water.

7. Remove scallop balls with slotted spoon and place on paper-towel-lined platter to drain. Cover loosely with foil to keep warm.

8. Combine remaining 6 cups stock, lemon rind and juice, and remaining ginger slice in large saucepan. Cover and bring to a boil over high heat.

9. Add mustard greens, coriander, and scallions, and allow stock to return to a boil. Add scallop balls and shrimp, reduce heat to medium-low, and cook 2 to 3 minutes, or until shrimp turn pink. Meanwhile, if using fish sauce or soy sauce, place in small serving bowl or pitcher.

10. Ladle soup into 4 individual bowls and garnish with lime quarters. Serve with fish sauce or soy sauce on the side, if desired.

Coriander-Shallot Chopstick Rolls

3 medium-size shallots
3 tablespoons unsalted butter

½ to 1 cup coarsely chopped coriander
8 egg-roll wrappers

1. Preheat oven to 350 degrees. Peel and mince shallots.
2. Melt 2 tablespoons butter in small skillet. Add shallots, and coriander to taste, and cook over medium-high heat 3 minutes, or until shallots are limp and coriander is wilted. Remove from heat and set aside.
3. Place egg-roll wrappers on flat surface. Spread 1 heaping tablespoon coriander-shallot mixture evenly over each egg-roll wrapper.
4. Roll up wrappers to enclose filling and place rolls, seam-side down, in 9-inch square baking pan.
5. In same small skillet, melt remaining tablespoon butter and brush chopstick rolls with melted butter.
6. Bake chopstick rolls 25 minutes, or until lightly browned.
7. Remove pan from oven and allow rolls to cool slightly in pan. Chopstick rolls will crisp as they cool.

Pineapple with Lime, Mint, and Red Pepper Flakes

Small bunch mint
Medium-size pineapple (3 to 3½ pounds)
2 tablespoons lime zest
3 tablespoons lime juice
2 tablespoons sugar
¼ to ½ teaspoon red pepper flakes
4 thin lime slices

1. Wash mint and dry with paper towels. Reserve 8 leaves for garnish and cut enough remaining mint into julienne strips to measure 3 tablespoons; refrigerate wrapped in paper towels until needed.
2. With chef's knife, cut ¾-inch slice from top and bottom of pineapple and discard. Pare pineapple, starting from top and following contours of pineapple with knife. With tip of paring knife, remove eyes. Cut 4 thin slices crosswise from center of pineapple and core slices. Core remaining pineapple and cut into chunks. Place pineapple in medium-size bowl, cover, and set aside until ready to serve.
3. In small nonaluminum saucepan, combine lime zest and juice, ½ cup water, sugar, and red pepper flakes to taste. Bring mixture to a boil over high heat. Continue to boil 3 to 5 minutes, or until syrup is reduced to ¼ cup. Remove from heat and let stand 2 to 3 minutes.
4. Place one pineapple slice on each of 4 dessert plates or in bowls. Top equally with pineapple chunks. Sprinkle with julienned mint, pour red pepper and lime syrup over each portion, and let stand until ready to serve.
5. Before serving, garnish with mint leaves and lime slices.

LEFTOVER SUGGESTION

Extra egg-roll wrappers can be used for *cannelloni*, or buttered, baked briefly in a hot oven, and served as canapé crackers.

Mock Mascarpone with Watercress
Mongolian Lamb and Vegetable Soup
Szechwan Pepper Buttons

Mock mascarpone *served with pumpernickel bread precedes the vegetable and lamb soup. Spicy butter cookies follow.*

The appetizer for this meal combines Brie, cream cheese, and butter to simulate Italian *mascarpone*—a thick, moist "double cream" cheese with a buttery flavor. The addition of watercress gives the cheese a mild bite.

The dessert cookies, spiced with Szechwan peppercorns, are a surprising finale for this ample dinner. Szechwan peppercorns are small brown kernels covered with a husk. They taste mildly hot and have a pungent aroma. To heighten their flavor, warm the peppercorns for a few moments in an ungreased pan over medium heat, shaking the pan frequently so the kernels do not burn. When they begin to release their oil, remove them from the heat.

WHAT TO DRINK

A medium-bodied dry white wine such as French Entre-Deux-Mers, or an Italian Soave or Orvieto, would complement this menu.

SHOPPING LIST AND STAPLES

1 pound boneless stewing lamb, in one piece
2 small carrots (about ⅓ pound total weight)
2 small turnips (about ⅓ pound total weight)
2 small zucchini (about ½ pound total weight)

2 small plum tomatoes (about ¼ pound total
   weight)
2 large onions (about 1 pound total weight)
8 medium-size cloves garlic
Medium-size bunch watercress
Small bunch parsley
1 lemon
6 tablespoons lightly salted butter
3 ounces ripe Brie
3-ounce package cream cheese
6 cups chicken stock, preferably homemade
   (see page 10), or canned
7 tablespoons vegetable oil
1 tablespoon soy sauce
1 tablespoon honey
Small loaf pumpernickel bread
½ cup all-purpose flour
2 tablespoons cornstarch
6 tablespoons confectioners' sugar
2 teaspoons mustard seeds
½ teaspoon whole Szechwan peppercorns, or
   black peppercorns
Salt
Freshly ground pepper
¼ cup dry sherry

UTENSILS

Food processor (optional)
Wok or large heavy-gauge skillet
Medium-size saucepan with cover
15 x 10-inch baking pan
15 x 10-inch baking sheet
8-inch square baking pan
Wire cooling rack
Large flat plate (if not using food processor)
Four 4-ounce ramekins
Medium-size bowl (if not using food processor)
Small strainer
Measuring cups and spoons
Chef's knife
Paring knife
Wooden spoon or wok spatula
2 metal spatulas
Slotted spoon
Rubber spatula
Ladle
Vegetable peeler

START-TO-FINISH STEPS

Thirty minutes ahead: Set out cream cheese, butter,
and Brie to come to room temperature for mascarpone
recipe.

1. Follow mascarpone recipe steps 1 and 2.
2. Follow soup recipe steps 1 through 6.
3. While vegetables bake, follow pepper buttons recipe
steps 1 through 3.

4. Follow soup recipe steps 7 through 9.
5. Follow mascarpone recipe steps 3 through 5 and serve
as first course.
6. Follow pepper buttons recipe step 4.
7. Follow soup recipe steps 10 through 12 and serve.
8. Follow pepper buttons recipe step 5 and serve for
dessert.

RECIPES

Mock Mascarpone with Watercress

Medium-size bunch watercress
3 ounces ripe Brie, at room temperature
3 ounces cream cheese, at room temperature
2 tablespoons lightly salted butter, at room
   temperature
6 slices pumpernickel bread

1. Wash watercress and dry with paper towels. Reserve 4
sprigs for garnish. Trim stems and finely chop enough
remaining watercress to measure ½ cup. Remove and
discard rind from Brie.

Watercress

2. In food processor fitted with steel blade, combine
watercress, Brie, cream cheese, and butter, and process
until smooth. Or, combine Brie, cream cheese, and butter
on large flat plate and cream together with fork. Gradually work in chopped watercress. Pack mixture into four
4-ounce ramekins; set aside.
3. Just before serving, place ramekins on center rack of
oven and bake until cheese is hot and melted, about 5 to 7
minutes.
4. Meanwhile, remove crusts from pumpernickel slices
and halve slices diagonally.
5. Remove ramekins from oven, garnish each with a
watercress sprig, and serve with pumpernickel.

Mongolian Lamb and Vegetable Soup

1 pound boneless stewing lamb, in one piece
8 medium-size cloves garlic
2 large onions (about 1 pound total weight)
2 small carrots (about ⅓ pound total weight)
2 small turnips (about ⅓ pound total weight)
2 small zucchini (about ½ pound total weight)
2 small plum tomatoes (about ¼ pound total weight)
Small bunch parsley
1 lemon
7 tablespoons vegetable oil

1 tablespoon honey
1 tablespoon soy sauce
6 cups chicken stock
2 teaspoons mustard seeds
¼ cup dry sherry
Salt
Freshly ground pepper

1. Preheat oven to 350 degrees.
2. Cut lamb into ¼-inch-thick slices. Crush and peel garlic. Halve and peel onions and cut crosswise into ¼-inch-thick slices; set aside.
3. Wash and dry vegetables, parsley, and lemon. Peel and coarsely chop carrots and turnips. Trim zucchini and cut lengthwise into ¼-inch-thick slices. Core tomatoes and cut into ¼-inch-thick slices. Mince enough parsley to measure 1 tablespoon. Cut lemon into wedges; set aside.
4. In 15 x 10-inch baking pan, combine 3 tablespoons oil, onion slices, and garlic cloves, and turn gently with spatula to coat with oil, being careful to keep onion slices intact.
5. In 8-inch square baking pan, combine 2 tablespoons oil, carrots, and turnips and stir to coat vegetables with oil.
6. Place both pans on middle rack of oven and bake vegetables 10 minutes.
7. Remove larger pan from oven and add zucchini to pan, turning carefully to coat slices with oil. Place tomatoes over zucchini, return pan to oven, and continue to bake both pans of vegetables 35 to 40 minutes, or until vegetables are tinged with brown.
8. Meanwhile, heat remaining 2 tablespoons oil in wok or large heavy-gauge skillet over high heat until hot. Add lamb and stir fry 3 minutes, or until slices are no longer pink.
9. Add honey and soy sauce to lamb and stir fry another 5 minutes, or until juices have evaporated and lamb is browned. Remove pan from heat and keep lamb warm on stove top.
10. In medium-size saucepan, combine stock, mustard seeds, and sherry. Cover pan and bring stock to a boil over high heat. Turn off heat and keep stock warm on stove top.
11. Using slotted spoon, transfer vegetables from both pans to large serving bowl or tureen.
12. Add ¼ cup hot stock to lamb and stir to deglaze pan. Transfer lamb and pan juices to saucepan with stock. Ladle stock and lamb over vegetables, season with salt and pepper to taste, and garnish soup with lemon wedges and minced parsley.

Szechwan Pepper Buttons

4 tablespoons lightly salted butter
6 tablespoons confectioners' sugar
½ cup all-purpose flour
2 tablespoons cornstarch
½ teaspoon whole Szechwan peppercorns, or black peppercorns

1. Cut butter into small pieces. In food processor, combine ¼ cup sugar, flour, and cornstarch. Process 1 second. Add butter and peppercorns and process until dough forms a ball. Or, combine ¼ cup sugar, flour, and cornstarch in medium-size bowl. Crush peppercorns under flat blade of chef's knife; add to bowl along with butter. Blend mixture with fingers until it holds together, then form dough into a ball.
2. Flatten ball and cut into 12 pieces. Roll pieces into 1-inch balls and place on 15 x 10-inch baking sheet.
3. Bake on upper rack of 350-degree oven 20 minutes, or until golden brown.
4. Remove cookies from oven, and while cookies are still warm on pan, sift remaining 2 tablespoons sugar over them. Transfer cookies to rack to cool.
5. Just before serving, transfer cookies to platter.

ADDED TOUCH

These deep-fried mint leaves are so crisp they shatter in the mouth, releasing their refreshing minty taste. The fried leaves become limp quickly in damp weather, so if you do not plan to eat them immediately, store them in an airtight container lined with paper towels, where they will keep for several days. Serve them as a unique appetizer or as a garnish for soups or stews.

Transparent Jade Mint Leaves

Large bunch mint
2 cups vegetable oil, approximately
Salt

1. Wash and dry mint. Remove 20 to 30 large leaves and reserve remaining mint for another use. Line platter with double thickness of paper towels.
2. In wok or large heavy-gauge skillet, heat oil until deep-fat thermometer registers 375 degrees.
3. Carefully drop a small handful of mint leaves into oil. Cook, turning often with mesh strainer, 5 to 10 seconds, or until leaves turn bright green and slightly transparent. Using slotted spoon, transfer leaves to paper-towel-lined platter to drain. Repeat for remaining leaves. As leaves cool, they become crisp and even more transparent.
4. Just before serving, salt leaves lightly.

Fresh mint

Donna Higgins

Donna Higgins, a California-based cook and recipe developer, enjoys preparing soups and stews for her family and friends because these dishes give her a great deal of latitude in the choice of ingredients and allow her to entertain as easily in the kitchen as in the dining room. She likes to experiment with soup and stew recipes, utilizing whatever she finds in the refrigerator and pantry.

The creamy broccoli-leek soup of Menu 3, for example, can be adapted to suit almost any vegetables. "I just let my imagination run wild," she says, "and use up whatever vegetables I have on hand." With the soup, Donna Higgins serves a light seafood salad on pineapple slices.

In Menu 1, she prepares a hearty lentil stew with chicken and sausage that is perfect fare for a chilly winter evening. The stew contains enough vegetables to make it almost a meal in itself. A tossed salad of chicory, lettuce, and orange segments accompanies the stew, and pineapple boats with strawberries and mint are served for dessert.

The seafood stew of Menu 2 is a quick version of the traditional long-simmering Mediterranean *bouillabaisse*. Almost any variety of seafood can be used in the stew as long as it is fresh from the market. Orzo pasta cooked in chicken stock and tossed with parsley is the side dish. The salad of avocado, papaya, tomatoes, and walnuts is refreshing with or after the meal.

For a winter dinner, offer rich lentil stew with sausage and chicken from a large tureen and a lightly dressed tossed salad as the accompaniment. Pineapple boats, served with fresh strawberries if they are available, make a refreshing dessert.

Savory Lentil Stew
Mixed Green and Citrus Salad
Pineapple Boats

Lentils, a primary ingredient in this savory stew, come in colors ranging from red to black. You can use any color lentils you like in this recipe if brown, ones are not available since the color does not affect the flavor greatly. Check the package directions, however, for slight variations in cooking time. Lentils require washing before use to remove any pebbles or other impurities, but they do not need presoaking.

Pineapples are sweet and juicy only when fully ripe; underripe pineapples are acidic and flavorless and will never sweeten or ripen even if held at room temperature for several days. Select a heavy pineapple with a golden-yellow rind and dark green crown leaves. It should have a rich fragrance.

WHAT TO DRINK

Either a California Gamay Beaujolais or a light beer or ale would go well with this uncomplicated meal.

SHOPPING LIST AND STAPLES

4 large pork link sausages, or 12 breakfast link sausages (about ¾ pound total weight)
6 medium-size chicken thighs (about 2 pounds total weight)
Small bunch celery
3 large carrots (about ¾ pound total weight)
Small bunch scallions
Small head chicory
Small head green or red leaf lettuce
2 medium-size yellow onions (about 1 pound total weight)
2 medium-size cloves garlic
Small bunch parsley
Small bunch mint
3 medium-size navel oranges
Large ripe pineapple (3 to 3½ pounds)
1 pint large strawberries, if available
3½ cups chicken stock, preferably homemade (see page 10), or canned
½ cup olive or vegetable oil
¼ cup red or white wine vinegar
½ teaspoon Dijon mustard
6 ounces brown lentils
2 teaspoons dried thyme
1 bay leaf
Salt

Freshly ground pepper
1 cup dry white wine
¼ cup Cointreau or kirsch

UTENSILS

Large heavy-gauge saucepan or flameproof casserole, with cover
Large skillet
Medium-size nonaluminum bowl
Salad spinner (optional)
Large strainer
Measuring cups and spoons
Chef's knife
Paring knife
Thin-bladed knife
Wooden spoon
Slotted spoon
Metal tongs
Vegetable peeler
Small jar with tight-fitting lid

START-TO-FINISH STEPS

1. Wash 1 orange. Using vegetable peeler or sharp paring knife, remove two 1-inch-long by ½-inch-wide strips of peel from orange for stew recipe. Peel and segment all 3 oranges, removing membranes and as much white pith as possible, over medium-size nonaluminum bowl to catch juice. Cover and refrigerate orange sections and juice for salad recipe.
2. Follow stew recipe steps 1 through 10.
3. While stew simmers, follow salad recipe steps 1 through 3 and pineapple recipe steps 1 through 3.
4. Follow salad recipe step 4, stew recipe step 11, and serve.
5. Follow pineapple recipe step 4 and serve for dessert.

RECIPES

Savory Lentil Stew

1 cup brown lentils
3½ cups chicken stock
2 teaspoons dried thyme
½ teaspoon salt
¼ teaspoon freshly ground pepper
1 bay leaf

Two 1-inch-long by ½-inch-wide strips orange peel
6 medium-size chicken thighs (about 2 pounds total weight)
4 large pork link sausages, or 12 breakfast link sausages (about ¾ pound total weight)
3 large carrots (about ¾ pound total weight)
2 medium-size yellow onions (about 1 pound total weight)
2 medium-size cloves garlic
4 medium-size stalks celery
1 cup dry white wine
Small bunch parsley

1. Wash lentils in large strainer under cold running water. In large heavy-gauge saucepan or flameproof casserole, combine lentils, stock, thyme, salt, pepper, bay leaf, and orange peel. Bring to a boil over high heat. Reduce heat to low, cover, and simmer 30 to 35 minutes, or until lentils are just tender.
2. Meanwhile, wash chicken thighs and dry with paper towels; set aside. Line platter with double thickness of paper towels. Prick sausages with tip of paring knife. Place sausages in large skillet and cook over medium-high heat 5 minutes, or until browned.
3. While sausages cook, wash, peel, and trim carrots and cut into very thin 1-inch julienne.
4. Using tongs, transfer sausages to paper-towel-lined platter to drain. Add chicken to skillet and cook over medium-high heat, turning occasionally, 6 to 8 minutes, or until browned on all sides.
5. While chicken cooks, peel and coarsely chop onions, crush and peel garlic, and wash, dry, and coarsely chop celery.
6. Using tongs, transfer chicken to paper-towel-lined platter to drain. Add carrots and celery to skillet and sauté, stirring, over medium-high heat, 3 to 4 minutes, or until softened. Add onions and garlic and continue to sauté another 3 to 4 minutes, or until onions are translucent.
7. With slotted spoon, transfer sautéed vegetables to pan or casserole with lentils. Drain off and discard any drippings remaining in skillet.
8. Increase heat under skillet to high, add wine to skillet, and bring to a boil, stirring to incorporate any brown bits clinging to bottom of pan. Cook 2 to 3 minutes, or until wine is slightly reduced.
9. Add reduced wine to lentils. Arrange chicken and sausages on top of lentils, cover, and simmer over medium-low heat 30 minutes.
10. Meanwhile, wash and dry parsley. Finely chop enough parsley to measure 1 tablespoon; reserve remainder for another use.
11. If using saucepan, turn stew into large serving bowl or tureen. Or, serve directly from casserole. Sprinkle with chopped parsley at the last minute.

Mixed Green and Citrus Salad

Small head chicory
Small head green or red leaf lettuce
3 large scallions
½ teaspoon Dijon mustard
⅛ teaspoon salt
Pinch of freshly ground pepper
¼ cup red or white wine vinegar
½ cup olive or vegetable oil
3 medium-size navel oranges, peeled and segmented, with juice

1. Wash chicory and lettuce and dry in salad spinner or with paper towels. Discard any bruised or discolored leaves. Tear chicory and lettuce into bite-size pieces. Place in plastic bag or wrap in paper towels and refrigerate until ready to serve.
2. Wash, trim, and thinly slice scallions; set aside.
3. For dressing, in small jar with tight-fitting lid, combine mustard, salt, pepper, and vinegar. Add oil, cover, and shake until well blended. Set aside.
4. Just before serving, combine salad greens, scallions, and orange sections in salad bowl. Sprinkle on any juice from oranges. Add dressing and toss until well coated.

Pineapple Boats

Large ripe pineapple (3 to 3½ pounds)
8 large fresh strawberries, if available
Small bunch mint
¼ cup Cointreau or kirsch

1. Leaving leafy crown attached, cut pineapple in half lengthwise with chef's knife. Cut each half lengthwise into 2 pieces.
2. Remove woody core and discard. Slide sharp, thin-bladed knife between flesh and rind to loosen flesh. Keeping fruit on shell, cut fruit lengthwise in half and then crosswise into bite-size pieces.

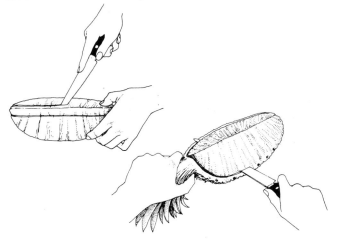

3. Rinse strawberries, if using, and pat dry with paper towels. Halve berries, leaving stems intact. Wash mint and pat dry with paper towels. Pinch off 4 or 5 mint sprigs for garnish.
4. To serve, pour 1 tablespoon Cointreau or kirsch over each pineapple boat and top with mint sprigs, and strawberry halves if using.

39

Seafood Stew
Avocado, Papaya, Tomato, and Walnut Salad
Orzo with Parsley

This succulent seafood stew includes monkfish and clams. Monkfish has a firm texture and does not disintegrate when cooked. Also marketed as goosefish or anglerfish, monkfish is popular on the Atlantic and Gulf coasts, but is less commonly available elsewhere in the country. If it is unavailable, use some other firm-fleshed white fish such as scrod or halibut.

When selecting live clams, make sure their shells are tightly closed: Those with slightly open or cracked shells may be old or dead. Also, do not buy any that feel un-

A meal that will satisfy family or friends, this informal feast includes a lusty seafood stew tinted with saffron, orzo with parsley, and a salad of avocado, papaya, tomatoes, and walnuts on a bed of watercress.

usually light or heavy in the shell. When storing unshucked clams, keep them dry in the coldest part of the refrigerator. Do not store them on ice.

The salad calls for a ripe papaya, a native Mexican fruit with a melon-like taste. Ripe papayas have yellow-orange skin and yield to gentle pressure. Ripen an immature papaya at room temperature and refrigerate it when it is soft if you do not intend to use it immediately. If you cannot find a papaya, use half a ripe cantaloupe instead.

WHAT TO DRINK

Try a fairly sturdy white wine with a personality of its own, such as a California Chardonnay or Pinot Blanc, or a French Chablis or Mâcon.

SHOPPING LIST AND STAPLES

½ pound monkfish fillets

½ pound salmon fillets, with skin attached

6 ounces fresh lump crabmeat, or 6 ounces medium-size shrimp, shelled and deveined

16 clams, in their shells (about 2 pounds total weight)

8 medium-size mushrooms (about 6 ounces total weight)

1 pint cherry tomatoes

Small bunch watercress

Medium-size onion

2 medium-size cloves garlic

Small bunch parsley

Large ripe avocado

Large ripe papaya

Large lemon

3 tablespoons unsalted butter

1 ounce Parmesan cheese

2 cups chicken stock, preferably homemade (see page 10), or canned

8-ounce bottle clam juice

14½-ounce can Italian plum tomatoes, or 1 pound fresh plum tomatoes plus ⅓ cup tomato juice

¼ cup olive oil

¼ cup vegetable oil

2 tablespoons walnut oil

2 tablespoons white wine vinegar

8-ounce package orzo

3-ounce package walnut halves

½ teaspoon dried basil

⅛ teaspoon fennel seeds

⅛ teaspoon saffron threads

Pinch of dry mustard

Salt and freshly ground white pepper

1 cup dry white wine

UTENSILS

Large heavy-gauge saucepan or flameproof casserole, with cover

Medium-size saucepan with cover

Small baking sheet

Small nonaluminum bowl

Colander

Measuring cups and spoons

Chef's knife

Paring knife

2 wooden spoons

Grater

Whisk

Ladle

Stiff-bristled brush

1. Follow salad recipe step 1.
2. Follow stew recipe steps 1 through 6.
3. While stew simmers, follow salad recipe steps 2 through 6.
4. Follow orzo recipe steps 1 and 2.
5. Follow stew recipe steps 7 through 9.
6. While stew continues to cook, follow orzo recipe step 3.
7. Follow salad recipe step 7, orzo recipe step 4, stew recipe step 10, and serve.

RECIPES

Seafood Stew

Medium-size onion
2 medium-size cloves garlic
8 medium-size mushrooms (about 6 ounces total weight)
16 clams, in their shells (about 2 pounds total weight)
¼ cup olive oil
14½-ounce can Italian plum tomatoes, or 1 pound fresh
    plum tomatoes plus ⅓ cup tomato juice
8-ounce bottle clam juice
1 cup dry white wine
½ teaspoon dried basil
⅛ teaspoon fennel seeds
⅛ teaspoon saffron threads
⅛ teaspoon freshly ground white pepper
½ pound monkfish fillets
½ pound salmon fillets, with skin attached
6 ounces fresh lump crabmeat, or 6 ounces medium-size
    shrimp, shelled and deveined

1. Peel and coarsely chop onion. Crush and peel garlic. Wipe mushrooms with damp paper towel and slice ⅛ inch thick; set aside.
2. Wash clams in several changes of cold water to remove grit. Scrub clams with stiff-bristled brush, rinse, and discard any clams with shells that are cracked or not tightly closed.
3. Heat oil in large heavy-gauge saucepan or flameproof casserole over medium heat. Add onion and cook 5 minutes, or until soft but not browned.
4. Meanwhile, coarsely chop tomatoes, reserving juice; set aside.
5. Add mushrooms and garlic to saucepan or casserole and cook, stirring, 3 minutes, or until softened.
6. Add tomatoes with their juice, clam juice, wine, basil, fennel seeds, saffron, and pepper. Bring to a boil over high heat. Reduce heat to low, cover, and simmer 30 minutes.
7. After liquid has simmered 30 minutes, add clams to saucepan, cover, and cook 5 minutes.
8. Meanwhile, wash fish and pat dry. Cut into bite-size pieces.
9. Add fish and crabmeat or shrimp to saucepan, cover, and simmer 10 minutes, or until clam shells open.
10. Discard any clams that have not opened. Ladle stew into tureen or divide among 4 individual bowls and serve.

Avocado, Papaya, Tomato, and Walnut Salad

Small bunch watercress
⅔ cup walnut halves
Large lemon
2 tablespoons white wine vinegar
⅛ teaspoon salt
Pinch of freshly ground white pepper
Pinch of dry mustard
¼ cup vegetable oil
2 tablespoons walnut oil
6 to 8 cherry tomatoes
Large ripe papaya
Large ripe avocado

1. Preheat oven to 350 degrees. Wash and dry watercress. Discard tough stem ends and damaged leaves. Place watercress in plastic bag and refrigerate until needed.
2. Spread walnuts on small baking sheet. Place in oven and toast, stirring occasionally, 5 to 7 minutes, or until lightly browned.
3. Meanwhile, juice lemon into small nonaluminum bowl. Add vinegar, salt, pepper, and dry mustard and stir to combine. Whisking constantly, add vegetable and walnut oils in a slow, steady stream and whisk until well blended.
4. Remove walnuts from oven and allow to cool. Wash and dry tomatoes and remove any stems. Halve tomatoes.
5. Halve papaya lengthwise and remove seeds. Cut each half lengthwise into 2 pieces and remove peel. Cut each quarter lengthwise into 3 or 4 thin slices.
6. Halve avocado lengthwise and remove pit. Cut each half lengthwise into 2 pieces and remove peel. Cut each quarter lengthwise into 3 thin slices. Place avocado slices on plate, drizzle with 2 tablespoons dressing, and turn slices to coat with dressing; set aside.
7. Just before serving, divide watercress among 4 individual salad plates. Arrange papaya and avocado slices decoratively over watercress. Garnish with cherry tomatoes and toasted walnuts. Spoon dressing over salad.

Orzo with Parsley

2 cups chicken stock
1 cup orzo
Small bunch parsley
1 ounce Parmesan cheese
3 tablespoons unsalted butter

1. In medium-size saucepan, bring 2 cups chicken stock and 1½ cups water to a boil over high heat. Add orzo and boil, uncovered, 10 to 15 minutes, or just until tender.
2. Meanwhile, wash and dry parsley. Coarsely chop enough parsley to measure ⅓ cup. Grate enough Parmesan to measure ¼ cup; set aside.
3. Turn cooked orzo into colander to drain briefly, then return to saucepan. Add parsley and butter and toss to combine. Cover pan and keep warm on stove top until ready to serve.
4. To serve, divide orzo among 4 individual bowls or small plates and sprinkle with grated Parmesan.

Shrimp and Scallop Salad
Creamy Broccoli-Leek Soup

The salad of shrimp and scallops on pineapple slices may be presented with or before the warming broccoli-leek soup.

You can turn this broccoli-leek soup into a green pepper soup by substituting 3 or 4 green peppers for the broccoli. Alternatively, make a lettuce soup by substituting 12 to 15 large outer leaves from 3 or 4 heads of romaine lettuce for the broccoli (save the inner leaves for a salad). Follow the method as directed.

For a dramatic chilled beet soup, substitute 1 pound of beets (3 to 4 medium beets) for the broccoli and omit the mushrooms and cheese. Pare and cut the beets into quarters, then cook them in the hot broth for 20 minutes. Purée the cooked beets in a food processor or blender and return the purée to the stockpot. Add ¼ teaspoon dried dill and simmer the mixture for 10 minutes. Sauté the leeks, then blend in the flour and cook 1 minute. Blend in 1 cup beet mixture and purée again. Add this mixture to the stockpot, and cook, stirring constantly, until thickened. Chill the soup thoroughly and serve it garnished with chopped chives and sour cream or *crème fraîche* (see page 18).

WHAT TO DRINK

A simple, somewhat fruity white wine would make a fine foil for the flavors in the vegetable soup. Try a dry California Chenin Blanc or an Italian Soave or Orvieto.

SHOPPING LIST AND STAPLES

6 ounces small shrimp, shelled, deveined, and cooked
6 ounces bay or sea scallops
Large bunch broccoli (about 1½ pounds)
3 large leeks (about 1 pound total weight)
6 large mushrooms (about 10 ounces total weight)
Small head leaf lettuce
Small bunch celery
Medium-size cucumber, zucchini,
    or green bell pepper
Small bunch scallions
Small bunch watercress or parsley (optional)
Medium-size pineapple (2½ to 3 pounds)
Large lemon (optional)
1 pint light cream or half-and-half
4 tablespoons unsalted butter
¼ pound Jarlsberg or Swiss cheese
4 cups chicken stock, preferably homemade (see page 10),
    or canned
½ cup mayonnaise, preferably homemade, or
    commercial
1 tablespoon Dijon mustard
¼ cup all-purpose flour
Salt
Freshly ground pepper
¼ cup dry white wine

UTENSILS

Food processor or blender
Large heavy-gauge nonaluminum stockpot or saucepan
Large skillet
Small nonaluminum skillet
2 medium-size bowls, 1 nonaluminum
Small bowl
Colander
Salad spinner (optional)
Measuring cups and spoons
Chef's knife
Paring knife
Wooden spoon
Slotted spoon
Rubber spatula
Grater
Whisk
Ladle

START-TO-FINISH STEPS

1. Follow salad recipe steps 1 through 5.
2. Follow soup recipe steps 1 through 4.
3. While soup simmers, follow salad recipe steps 6 and 7.
4. Follow soup recipe steps 5 though 8 and serve with salad.

RECIPES

Shrimp and Scallop Salad

6 ounces small shrimp, shelled, deveined, and
    cooked
6 ounces bay or sea scallops
¼ cup dry white wine
Small head leaf lettuce
Medium-size cucumber, zucchini, or green
    bell pepper
3 large scallions
2 large stalks celery
½ cup mayonnaise, preferably homemade,
    or commercial
1 tablespoon Dijon mustard
Medium-size pineapple (2½ to 3 pounds)
Small bunch watercress or parsley for
    garnish (optional)
Large lemon (optional)

1. Rinse shrimp and scallops in colander under cold running water and pat dry with paper towels. If large, cut scallops into ½-inch pieces.
2. In small nonaluminum skillet, bring wine to a simmer over medium heat. Add scallops and poach 5 minutes, or until opaque. Using slotted spoon, transfer scallops to small bowl and place in refrigerator to chill. Increase heat under skillet to high and boil wine 5 minutes, or until reduced to 1 tablespoon; set aside.
3. Meanwhile, wash lettuce and dry in salad spinner or with paper towels. Select enough large, unblemished leaves to line 4 salad plates, place in plastic bag, and refrigerate until needed. Reserve remaining lettuce for another use.
4. Wash and dry remaining vegetables. Halve, seed, and coarsely chop cucumber, zucchini, or bell pepper. Trim scallions and cut into ¼-inch-thick slices. Cut celery into ¼-inch-thick slices.
5. In medium-size nonaluminum bowl, combine reduced

wine with mayonnaise and mustard and blend well with fork. Add shrimp, scallops, cucumber, zucchini, or bell pepper, scallions, and celery and mix until well combined; set aside.

6. With chef's knife, trim crown and stem end from pineapple. Cut pineapple crosswise into ¾-inch-thick slices. Trim rind from each slice and remove core. Wash and dry watercress or parsley, if using, and set aside 4 sprigs for garnish.

7. Line 4 salad plates with lettuce leaves. Place 1 pineapple slice on each plate and top with seafood mixture. If using lemon, cut into 8 wedges and place 2 wedges on each salad. Garnish with watercress or parsley sprigs, if desired.

Creamy Broccoli-Leek Soup

4 cups chicken stock
Large bunch broccoli (about 1½ pounds)
3 large leeks (about 1 pound total weight)
6 large mushrooms (about 10 ounces total weight)
¼ pound Jarlsberg or Swiss cheese
4 tablespoons unsalted butter
¼ cup all-purpose flour
1½ cups light cream or half-and-half
Salt
Freshly ground pepper

1. In large heavy-gauge nonaluminum stockpot or saucepan, bring stock to a boil over high heat.
2. Meanwhile, wash broccoli and cut into florets. Peel large stems and cut into ½-inch-thick pieces. Add florets and stems to boiling stock and cook, uncovered, 15 minutes, or until tender.
3. While broccoli cooks, trim leeks, discarding green tops. Cut leeks in half lengthwise and wash carefully under cold running water to remove all sand and grit. Thinly slice leeks. Wipe mushrooms clean with damp paper towels and cut into ¼-inch-thick slices. Finely grate cheese; set aside.
4. When broccoli is cooked, remove from stock with slotted spoon. Set aside 4 florets for garnish. Place half of remaining broccoli in food processor fitted with steel blade or in blender. Add ½ cup hot stock and process until puréed. Transfer purée to medium-size bowl. Purée remaining broccoli with ½ cup hot stock. Return both batches of purée to stockpot, stir, and simmer soup over low heat 10 minutes.

5. In large skillet, melt butter over medium heat. Add leeks and mushrooms and sauté 5 minutes, or until leeks are soft but not browned. Whisk in flour and cook, stirring, 1 minute. Remove skillet from heat.
6. Working quickly, whisk 2 cups simmering soup into mixture in skillet and stir to combine. Return mixture to stockpot and bring to a boil over medium heat. Cook, stirring constantly, 3 to 4 minutes, or until soup is thickened.
7. Reduce heat to low and stir in cream or half-and-half; do not allow soup to boil.
8. Just before serving, stir in grated cheese, and season soup with salt and pepper to taste. Ladle soup into 4 individual bowls and garnish each with a broccoli floret.

ADDED TOUCH

Molasses cookies can burn easily, so keep an eye on them.

Molasses Sugar Cookies

2 cups sifted all-purpose flour
2 teaspoons baking soda
1 teaspoon cinnamon
½ teaspoon ground cloves
½ teaspoon ground ginger
½ teaspoon salt
¾ cup shortening
1½ cups sugar
¼ cup dark molasses
1 egg, at room temperature

1. In large bowl, sift together flour, baking soda, cinnamon, cloves, ginger, and salt; set aside.
2. With electric mixer, cream together shortening and 1 cup sugar in medium-size bowl. Add molasses and egg and beat until well blended. Add flour mixture and mix well. Form dough into ball and divide in half. Wrap each half in plastic wrap and refrigerate at least 30 minutes.
3. Preheat oven to 375 degrees.
4. Grease 2 medium-size cookie sheets.
5. Place remaining ½ cup sugar in shallow bowl. Remove half of dough from refrigerator. Shape dough into approximately twenty-four 1-inch balls. Roll each ball in sugar and place 2 inches apart on cookie sheets.
6. Bake cookies 8 to 10 minutes, or until golden brown. Let stand on cookie sheets 1 minute. Remove to wire rack to cool.
7. Repeat for remaining cookie dough.

Beatrice Ojakangas

MENU 1 (Right)
Finnish Summer Soup
Smoked Salmon and Egg Smörrebröd
Tomato and Enoki Mushroom Salad

MENU 2
Red and White Soup
Pasties with Mustard Butter
Creamy Havarti and Vegetable Salad

MENU 3
Hearty Beef, Barley, and Wild Rice Stew
with Finnish Raisin Dumplings
Scandinavian Salad

A resident of a Scandinavian community in Minnesota, Beatrice Ojakangas is proud of her Finnish heritage. Not surprisingly, her favorite cuisine is from Scandinavia, and she has traveled there to master traditional recipes and techniques. The three menus she presents here span the seasons. Menu 1 features a delicate Finnish summer soup known as *kesäkeitto*, which is made with baby carrots, new potatoes, and young green beans. "In Finland, this produce is in abundance only during the intense summers, when the sun shines 24 hours a day," she says. She is delighted that many American markets now carry baby vegetables all year round.

The thick red and white soup of Menu 2 is more autumnal, using red bell pepper, fresh tomatoes, potatoes, and leeks. An attractive vegetable and cheese salad and flaky turnovers called pasties (pronounced *past*-ees), filled with a savory mixture of sausage, beef, and seasonings, are served with the soup.

Menu 3 is a hearty winter meal reflecting both Swedish and Finnish influences. Beef, onions, mushrooms, barley, and wild rice simmer in a stock, melding to create a rich flavorful stew. Finnish raisin dumplings, an old-country classic, steam with the stew, and a colorful vegetable salad is the refreshing accompaniment.

Celebrate summer with a large bowl of hot Finnish soup made with a variety of colorful vegetables. An open-faced sandwich of smoked salmon topped with cheese soufflé, and a simple tomato and mushroom salad, are appealing partners for the soup.

Finnish Summer Soup
Smoked Salmon and Egg Smörrebröd
Tomato and Enoki Mushroom Salad

The *smörrebröd*, which literally means "buttered bread" in Danish, has as its base slices of pumpernickel, which should be buttered thickly and evenly to seal the bread from the juices in the toppings. Toppings for *smörrebröd* can consist of almost any foods that look and taste good together. For this version, the cook uses colorful smoked salmon and a simple soufflé containing Danish Edam cheese. Purchase top-quality salmon and use it as soon as possible, since it deteriorates quickly. If desired, you can add two chopped hard-boiled eggs to the salmon mixture.

The sliced tomatoes are crowned with *enoki* (or *enokitaki*) mushrooms—slender, ivory-colored stalks that look like tiny umbrellas. These mushrooms are increasingly available in well-stocked supermarkets, specialty food stores, and Oriental groceries. Refrigerate them in the original package or wrapped in paper towels for a day or two. You can substitute fresh button mushrooms or chanterelles for the *enoki*.

WHAT TO DRINK

In Scandinavia, this summer soup would be accompanied by a well-chilled light beer, but crisp white wine is also appropriate. Consider a California Sauvignon Blanc or a French Sancerre.

SHOPPING LIST AND STAPLES

¾ pound smoked salmon, in one piece
Medium-size head cauliflower (about 2 pounds)
2 large ripe tomatoes (about 1½ pounds total weight)
8 small new red potatoes (about ¾ pound total weight)
¾ pound baby carrots, or 3 medium-size carrots
¾ pound fresh green peas, or 9-ounce package frozen
¼ pound fresh snow peas
2 ounces small fresh green beans
Large head butter lettuce
Small bunch fresh spinach (optional)
¼ pound fresh enoki mushrooms
Small white onion (about ¼ pound)
Small bunch chives
Small bunch parsley
Large lemon
2 eggs
1 pint half-and-half
½ pint sour cream

6 tablespoons unsalted butter, approximately
¼ pound Danish Edam cheese
4 cups chicken stock, preferably homemade (see page 10), or canned (optional)
¼ cup vegetable oil
2 tablespoons white wine vinegar
3 tablespoons mayonnaise
2 teaspoons Dijon mustard
2 tablespoons all-purpose flour
2 teaspoons sugar
Small loaf pumpernickel bread
Salt and freshly ground white pepper

UTENSILS

Electric mixer (optional)
Large stockpot with cover
Small deep saucepan
15 x 10-inch baking sheet
Medium-size bowl
3 small bowls, 1 nonaluminum
Colander
Measuring cups and spoons
Chef's knife
Paring knife
2 wooden spoons
Grater
Whisk
Metal spatula
Rubber spatula
Vegetable peeler
Ladle

START-TO-FINISH STEPS

Thirty minutes ahead: Set out eggs and 4 teaspoons butter to come to room temperature for smörrebröd recipe.

1. Follow soup recipe steps 1 through 3 and smörrebröd recipe steps 1 through 5.
2. Follow salad recipe step 1 and soup recipe steps 4 through 6.
3. Follow salad recipe steps 2 and 3 and smörrebröd recipe steps 6 and 7.
4. While smörrebröd bake, follow salad recipe steps 4 through 6 and soup recipe step 7.
5. Follow smörrebröd recipe step 8, soup recipe step 8, and serve with salad.

RECIPES

Finnish Summer Soup

Medium-size head cauliflower (about 2 pounds)
¾ pound baby carrots, or 3 medium-size carrots
8 small new red potatoes (about ¾ pound total weight)
Small white onion (about ¼ pound)
2 teaspoons salt
4 cups chicken stock or water, approximately
¾ pound fresh green peas, or 9-ounce package frozen
¼ pound fresh snow peas
2 ounces small fresh green beans
2 cups half-and-half
2 tablespoons all-purpose flour
4 tablespoons unsalted butter
1 teaspoon sugar
⅛ teaspoon freshly ground white pepper
Small bunch fresh spinach for garnish (optional)

1. Trim and discard stem and leaves from cauliflower. Wash cauliflower and separate into florets; cut florets into 1-inch pieces. You should have about 8 cups. Peel and trim carrots; cut carrots crosswise, if necessary, into 2½- to 3-inch pieces. Wash and peel potatoes; cut into quarters. Peel onion and cut into 8 wedges.
2. In large stockpot, combine cauliflower, carrots, potatoes, onion, salt, and enough stock or water to barely cover vegetables. Cover and bring to a boil over high heat. Reduce heat and simmer vegetables 15 minutes, or until just tender but not mushy.
3. Meanwhile, shell enough fresh peas, if using, to measure 1½ cups. If using frozen peas, remove from freezer and separate enough peas to measure 1½ cups; do not thaw first. Wash, trim, and string snow peas. Wash and trim green beans; cut into 1-inch pieces.
4. Add peas, snow peas, green beans, and 1 cup half-and-half to stockpot. Simmer over low heat 3 minutes.
5. Meanwhile, in small bowl, combine remaining 1 cup half-and-half with flour and beat until smooth. Stir mixture into simmering soup and cook, stirring occasionally, 1 to 2 minutes, or until soup is slightly thickened.
6. Cut butter into small pieces and add to soup along with sugar and pepper. Keep soup warm over very low heat until ready to serve; do not let soup boil.
7. Wash enough spinach, if using, to measure ⅓ cup; reserve remaining spinach for another use. Trim stems and cut spinach leaves into ½-inch-wide ribbons. Set aside for garnish.
8. To serve, divide soup among 4 bowls and top with spinach leaves, if desired.

Smoked Salmon and Egg Smörrebröd

¾ pound smoked salmon, in one piece
3 tablespoons mayonnaise
3 tablespoons sour cream
Large lemon
Small loaf pumpernickel bread

4 teaspoons unsalted butter, at room temperature
¼ pound Danish Edam cheese
2 eggs, at room temperature
Small bunch parsley

1. Preheat oven to 375 degrees.
2. Remove skin and bones, if necessary, from salmon. Flake fish into small bowl. Add mayonnaise and sour cream and stir with fork until well blended.
3. Wash lemon. Using vegetable peeler or paring knife, remove four 2-inch-wide strips of lemon peel and reserve for garnish. Halve lemon and squeeze enough juice to measure ¼ cup; stir juice into salmon mixture.
4. Cut four ½-inch-thick slices of pumpernickel and spread each slice with 1 teaspoon softened butter.
5. Spread pumpernickel slices with salmon mixture. Place slices on 15 x 10-inch baking sheet; set aside.
6. Using grater, finely shred cheese. Separate eggs, placing whites in medium-size bowl and reserving yolks for another use. Using electric mixer or whisk, beat egg whites until stiff. Using rubber spatula, fold in shredded cheese. Spread mixture equally over salmon.
7. Bake smörrebröd 10 to 15 minutes, or until topping is golden.
8. Just before serving, wash and dry parsley. Cut 4 sprigs for garnish and reserve remainder for another use. Place 1 smörrebröd on each of 4 dinner plates and garnish each with a parsley sprig and a strip of lemon peel.

Tomato and Enoki Mushroom Salad

Large head butter lettuce
Small bunch chives
2 large ripe tomatoes (about 1½ pounds total weight)
2 teaspoons Dijon mustard
2 tablespoons white wine vinegar
1 teaspoon sugar
¼ teaspoon salt
¼ cup vegetable oil
¼ pound fresh enoki mushrooms

1. Bring 1 quart water to a boil in small deep saucepan over high heat.
2. Wash and dry lettuce and chives. Wrap lettuce in paper towels or plastic bag and refrigerate until needed. Finely chop enough chives to measure ¼ cup; set aside.
3. Immerse tomatoes in boiling water 30 seconds. Turn tomatoes into colander and refresh under cold running water. Peel tomatoes and set aside.
4. In small nonaluminum bowl, whisk together mustard, vinegar, sugar, and salt. Stir in chopped chives. Whisking constantly, add oil in a slow, steady stream, and whisk until smooth.
5. Wipe mushrooms with damp paper towel and trim stem ends. Add to dressing and toss gently to coat. Core tomatoes and cut each crosswise into 4 slices.
6. To serve, line 4 salad plates with lettuce leaves. Place 2 tomato slices on each plate and top with mushrooms and dressing.

Red and White Soup
Pasties with Mustard Butter
Creamy Havarti and Vegetable Salad

Serving two contrasting soups in one bowl is a sure way to delight guests. Offer the pasties before, with, or after the soup and salad.

The unusual cold soup is actually two soups in one. To ensure that they remain separate, use shallow bowls and pour both soups carefully into the bowls at the same time. The soup is as good hot as cold.

When baking the pasties, line the baking pans with kitchen parchment (available in kitchen supply stores) to aid in even browning. Brown wrapping paper makes an adequate substitute. The pasties can be served hot or at room temperature.

WHAT TO DRINK

Beer, ale, or a California Zinfandel or Petite Sirah would be a good choice for this light supper.

SHOPPING LIST AND STAPLES

½ pound lean ground beef
¼ pound seasoned pork sausage
3 large ripe tomatoes (about 1½ pounds total weight)
3 medium-size boiling potatoes (about 1 pound total weight)
Large head butter, Boston, or Bibb lettuce
Small head red cabbage
Small head cauliflower
Large leek
Large red bell pepper
Medium-size yellow onion
Medium-size clove garlic
Small bunch fresh basil, or 1 teaspoon dried
1 cup milk
½ pint heavy cream
2 sticks unsalted butter, approximately
¼ pound creamy Havarti cheese
½ pint creamed small curd cottage cheese
4 cups chicken stock, preferably homemade (see page 10), or canned
¼ cup plus 2 tablespoons vegetable oil
2 tablespoons white wine vinegar
¼ cup coarse-grain mustard
2 teaspoons Dijon mustard
1¼ cups all-purpose flour
1 teaspoon sugar
2 tablespoons cornstarch
¼ cup walnut or pecan pieces
1 tablespoon fine dry bread crumbs
½ teaspoon dried thyme
¼ teaspoon ground allspice
Salt
Freshly ground white pepper

UTENSILS

Food processor or blender
2 large heavy-gauge saucepans with covers
Small saucepan
17 x 11-inch baking sheet
3 large bowls, plus 1 bowl (optional)
Medium-size bowl
Small nonaluminum bowl
Measuring cups and spoons
Chef's knife
Paring knife
2 wooden spoons
Metal spatula
Rubber spatula
Whisk
Rolling pin
Pastry blender (if not using food processor)
Vegetable peeler
Parchment paper or brown wrapping paper

START-TO-FINISH STEPS

1. Follow soup recipe steps 1 through 4.
2. While soups are simmering, follow pasties recipe steps 1 through 3.
3. While dough is chilling, follow salad recipe steps 1 through 3.
4. Follow soup recipe steps 5 and 6.
5. While soups are chilling, follow pasties recipe steps 4 through 9.
6. While pasties are baking, follow salad recipe steps 4 through 6.
7. Follow pasties recipe step 10, soup recipe step 7, and serve with salad.

RECIPES

Red and White Soup

Medium-size yellow onion
Medium-size clove garlic
Large leek
Large red bell pepper
3 medium-size boiling potatoes (about 1 pound total weight)
3 large ripe tomatoes (about 1½ pounds total weight)
Small bunch fresh basil, or 1 teaspoon dried
3 tablespoons unsalted butter
4 cups chicken stock
2 tablespoons cornstarch
Salt
Freshly ground white pepper
1 cup milk
½ cup heavy cream

1. Peel onion and garlic; coarsely chop both and set aside. Cut off and discard dark green leaves of leek. Trim root end, split leek lengthwise, and wash well under cold running water; dry with paper towel. Coarsely chop leek and set aside. Wash and dry red bell pepper. Halve, core, and seed pepper; chop coarsely and set aside. Peel potatoes and cut into coarse dice; set aside. Wash, core, and coarsely chop tomatoes; set aside.
2. Wash and dry fresh basil, if using. Set aside 4 sprigs for garnish and coarsely chop enough basil to measure 1 table-

spoon; set aside. Reserve remaining basil for another use.

3. In large heavy-gauge saucepan, melt 2 tablespoons butter over medium heat. Add onion and garlic and sauté 1 minute, or until soft but not browned. Add bell pepper and tomatoes and sauté 2 to 3 minutes, stirring once or twice, until heated through but not browned. Add 2 cups stock, cover, and simmer about 20 minutes, or until vegetables are tender.

4. Meanwhile, in another large heavy-gauge saucepan, melt remaining tablespoon butter over medium heat. Add leek and sauté 1 minute, or until soft but not browned. Add potatoes and sauté 2 to 3 minutes, stirring once or twice, until heated through but not browned. Add remaining 2 cups stock, cover, and simmer about 20 minutes, or until vegetables are tender.

5. Pour bell pepper and tomato mixture into food processor fitted with steel blade, or blender, and purée until almost smooth. Add cornstarch and continue processing until smooth. Return soup to pan, bring to a simmer over medium heat, and cook, stirring, 2 to 3 minutes, or until soup thickens. Stir in chopped or dried basil, and salt and pepper to taste. Transfer soup to large bowl and chill in refrigerator at least 20 minutes, or until ready to serve.

6. Rinse out processor or blender and turn potato mixture into it. Process until puréed and smooth (the potato soup should be of the same consistency as the pepper soup). Stir in milk and cream, and salt and pepper to taste. Transfer soup to large bowl and chill in refrigerator at least 20 minutes, or until ready to serve.

7. To serve, stir each chilled soup to ensure smoothness. Taste, and adjust seasonings. Using 2 cups, simultaneously pour 1 cup of each soup into shallow soup bowl so that red soup is on one side and white soup is on the other side. (The equal density of the two soups keeps them from running together.) Fill remaining 3 soup bowls in same manner. Garnish each with a basil sprig.

Pasties with Mustard Butter

1¼ cups all-purpose flour
1 stick plus 4 tablespoons unsalted butter, well chilled
½ cup creamed small curd cottage cheese
¼ pound seasoned pork sausage
½ pound lean ground beef
1 tablespoon fine dry bread crumbs
½ teaspoon salt
½ teaspoon dried thyme
¼ teaspoon ground allspice
¼ cup coarse-grain mustard

1. Prepare pastry: Place flour in food processor fitted with steel blade. Cut 1 stick butter into small pieces and add to flour. Process, pulsing on and off 8 to 10 times, until mixture is in pea-size pieces. Add cottage cheese and pulse 10 to 15 times, or until dough holds together in a ball. (If mixture is too dry to form a ball, add 1 tablespoon cold water.) To make pastry by hand, add cut-up butter to flour in large bowl and blend with pastry blender or 2 knives until mixture is in pea-size pieces. Add cottage cheese and

stir with wooden spoon until dough holds together, adding 1 tablespoon cold water, if necessary. Remove dough from processor or bowl and flatten into a disk. Wrap dough in plastic and refrigerate 10 minutes.

2. Meanwhile, in medium-size bowl, combine sausage, beef, bread crumbs, salt, thyme, and allspice, and stir until well blended.

3. Preheat oven to 450 degrees.

4. Lightly dust rolling pin with flour. Place dough on lightly floured surface and roll out pastry to ¼-inch thickness. Trim dough to 10 x 20-inch rectangle and cut into eight 5-inch squares.

5. Divide meat mixture into eight equal portions. Spread one portion on one triangular half of each square, leaving a narrow border.

6. Fold pastry squares diagonally in half to make triangular pasties, pressing down to flatten slightly. Crimp edges with tines of fork. Cut 3 slits on top of each pasty with tip of knife to allow steam to escape.

7. Line 17 x 11-inch baking sheet with parchment paper or brown wrapping paper. Using metal spatula, transfer pasties to parchment.

8. Bake pasties 15 minutes, or until golden.

9. Meanwhile, melt remaining 4 tablespoons butter in small saucepan. Add mustard and stir to blend. Pour into 4 small ramekins or one small serving bowl.

10. Using metal spatula, transfer 2 pasties to each of 4 plates and serve with mustard butter on the side.

Creamy Havarti and Vegetable Salad

Small head red cabbage
Small head cauliflower
¼ pound creamy Havarti cheese
Large head butter, Boston, or Bibb lettuce
2 teaspoons Dijon mustard
1 teaspoon sugar
2 tablespoons white wine vinegar
¼ cup plus 2 tablespoons vegetable oil
Salt and freshly ground pepper
¼ cup walnut or pecan pieces

1. Wash, halve, and core cabbage. Cut enough cabbage into medium-size shreds to measure about 6 cups; place in large bowl. Reserve remaining cabbage for another use.

2. Trim stem and leaves from cauliflower. Wash cauliflower and break enough into ½-inch florets to measure about 2 cups; add to bowl.

3. Cut cheese into ¼-inch-thick by 2-inch-long pieces and add to bowl; set aside.

4. Wash lettuce and dry with paper towels. Arrange 3 or 4 leaves on each of 4 dinner plates or line 4 salad plates with leaves.

5. For dressing, in small nonaluminum bowl, whisk together mustard, sugar, and vinegar. Whisking constantly, add oil in a slow, steady stream and whisk until smooth. Season with salt and pepper to taste.

6. To serve, pour dressing over vegetables and cheese and toss to coat. Spoon onto lettuce and sprinkle with nuts.

Hearty Beef, Barley, and Wild Rice Stew
with Finnish Raisin Dumplings
Scandinavian Salad

A colorful vegetable salad with creamy dressing is an attractive complement to the beef stew with dumplings.

The substantial stew calls for an American native— wild rice. The seeds of a wild grass, wild rice is painstakingly harvested by hand, hence it is costly, but well worth the price. Fortunately, a little goes a long way.

The cook also uses whole allspice berries to flavor the stew. These dried unripe berries of the West Indian allspice tree taste like a combination of cloves, cinnamon, and nutmeg and are most flavorful in their unground state.

WHAT TO DRINK

This cold-weather meal demands a sturdy drink: Select a dark ale or a young California Zinfandel.

SHOPPING LIST AND STAPLES

1 pound boneless sirloin or top round steak, trimmed
3 medium-size beets (about 1¼ pounds total weight)
3 medium-size carrots (about ½ pound total weight)
3 medium-size boiling potatoes (about 1 pound total weight)
½ pound fresh mushrooms
2 large onions (about 1½ pounds total weight)
Small bunch scallions
Small bunch fresh parsley
Small bunch fresh dill, or 1 teaspoon dried
2 medium-size Granny Smith apples (about 1 pound total weight)
Small lemon
1 egg
½ cup milk
½ pint heavy cream
4 tablespoons unsalted butter
4 cups beef stock, preferably homemade (see page 10), or canned
16-ounce jar dill pickles
1 tablespoon vegetable oil
4-ounce package wild rice
¼ cup pearl barley
1 cup all-purpose flour
1 teaspoon baking powder
2 teaspoons sugar
½ cup dark raisins
3 whole allspice berries
¼ teaspoon ground allspice
Salt

UTENSILS

Electric mixer
Large stockpot with cover
Medium-size saucepan
Small saucepan
Large bowl
Medium-size bowl
Small bowl
Colander
Strainer
Measuring cups and spoons
Chef's knife
Paring knife
2 wooden spoons
Ladle

START-TO-FINISH STEPS

1. Follow salad recipe steps 1 and 2.
2. While vegetables cook, follow stew recipe steps 1 through 6.
3. While stew simmers, follow salad recipe steps 3 through 8.
4. Follow stew recipe steps 7 through 10 and salad recipe step 9.
5. Follow stew recipe step 11 and serve with salad.

RECIPES

Hearty Beef, Barley, and Wild Rice Stew with Finnish Raisin Dumplings

⅓ cup wild rice
2 large onions (about 1½ pounds total weight)
4 tablespoons unsalted butter
¼ cup pearl barley
1 pound boneless sirloin or top round steak, trimmed
3 whole allspice berries
4 cups beef stock
½ pound fresh mushrooms
Small bunch parsley

Finnish Raisin Dumplings:
1 egg
1 tablespoon vegetable oil
½ cup milk
1 cup all-purpose flour

1 teaspoon baking powder
½ teaspoon salt
¼ teaspoon ground allspice
½ cup dark raisins

1. Place wild rice in small bowl. Add hot tap water to cover and stir; drain in strainer. Repeat until soaking water is clear. Drain.
2. Peel onions and slice ¼-inch thick; set aside.
3. Melt butter in large stockpot over medium heat. Add wild rice and barley and stir to coat with butter.
4. Add onions to rice and barley and stir to separate onion slices into rings. Simmer 3 to 5 minutes, or until onions begin to soften.
5. Meanwhile, cut steak into ¼-inch-thick slices. Cut slices crosswise into 1-inch pieces. Add steak and allspice berries to stockpot and increase heat to high. Cook, stirring, 5 minutes, or until meat is no longer pink.
6. Add stock and bring to a boil. Reduce heat, cover, and simmer 30 minutes, or until meat is tender and rice and barley are cooked.
7. Wipe mushrooms clean with damp paper towel. Cut mushrooms into ¼-inch-thick slices; set aside. Wash and dry parsley. Chop enough parsley to measure 2 teaspoons; set aside. Reserve remainder for another use.
8. Combine all raisin dumpling ingredients in large bowl. Stir until dry ingredients are just moistened.
9. Dip a tablespoon into stew cooking liquid to moisten, then scoop up a rounded spoonful of dumpling batter. Drop batter into stew; repeat for remaining batter. You should have about 15 dumplings.
10. Add mushrooms to stew, cover, and simmer 5 minutes. Stir gently, cover, and cook another 5 to 7 minutes, or until dumplings are fluffy and no longer doughy underneath.
11. Sprinkle stew with parsley and serve directly from stockpot. Or, ladle stew into 4 soup bowls.

Scandinavian Salad

3 medium-size beets (about 1¼ pounds total weight)
3 medium-size carrots (about ½ pound total weight)
3 medium-size boiling potatoes (about 1 pound total weight)
4 large dill pickles
Small lemon
2 medium-size Granny Smith apples (about 1 pound total weight)

4 scallions
Small bunch fresh dill, or 1 teaspoon dried
1 cup heavy cream
2 teaspoons sugar
½ teaspoon salt

1. Place medium-size bowl and beaters in freezer to chill.
2. Wash beets, being careful not to damage skin. Trim stems, if any, no closer than 2 inches; do not trim bottoms. Wash carrots and potatoes. Place beets in small saucepan and add water to cover. Place carrots and potatoes in medium-size saucepan and add water to cover. Bring water in both pans to a boil over high heat. Reduce heat to low and simmer vegetables 15 to 20 minutes, or until slightly tender but still firm.
3. Cut dill pickles into ½-inch dice and arrange in one corner of large platter. Halve lemon and squeeze enough juice to measure at least 4 teaspoons; set aside. Core, but do not peel, apples. Cut apples into ½-inch dice and sprinkle with 1 teaspoon lemon juice. Arrange apples in diagonal row next to pickles. Wash and trim scallions. Cut scallions crosswise into ¼-inch slices; set aside. Wash and dry fresh dill, if using. Set aside 1 sprig for garnish, and finely chop enough dill to measure 1 tablespoon; set aside. Reserve remaining dill for another use.
4. For dressing, in chilled medium-size bowl, whip cream. Add remaining tablespoon lemon juice, sugar, salt, and chopped or dried dill. Blend in 2 teaspoons beet cooking liquid to tint dressing slightly. (If dressing seems pale, add ¼ teaspoon finely chopped beet after beets are cooked to tint it more deeply.) Turn dressing into small serving bowl.
5. When beets are tender, drain in colander, return to pan, and cover with cold water. Let stand 2 to 3 minutes, or until cool enough to handle.
6. Meanwhile, drain carrots and potatoes, return to pan, and cover with cold water.
7. When beets are cool, trim tops and root ends and slip off skins. Cut beets into ½-inch dice and arrange in diagonal row next to apples on platter.
8. When carrots and potatoes are cool, peel and cut both into ½-inch dice. Arrange potatoes in diagonal row next to beets on platter, and arrange carrots in same manner next to potatoes.
9. Sprinkle narrow band of chopped scallions between rows of vegetables. Garnish dressing with dill sprig and serve with salad.

Laurie Goldrich

Although Laurie Goldrich has prepared many ethnic meals in her lifetime, she favors southern cooking—particularly the one-pot dishes of Louisiana's Creole cuisine—over all. Inspired by French, Spanish, and African cuisines, Creole cooking consists largely of highly seasoned yet subtle and elegant seafood and vegetable dishes.

To showcase this original and eclectic way of cooking, Laurie Goldrich offers three well-known Creole main courses, beginning in Menu 1 with beef *grillades*, a traditional New Orleans dish generally served at breakfast or brunch and accompanied by grits. *Grillade* is a French word meaning "grilled meat." *Grillades* are generally made with tougher cuts of beef or veal, which become tender when braised at length in a thick sauce. This menu calls for beef tenderloin tips and quick-cooking grits to save time.

Gumbo is the featured dish of Menu 2. Although there is no hard and fast recipe for gumbo, this soup-stew usually contains a variety of meats, seafood, and vegetables. Here chicken parts, spicy *andouille* sausage, and fresh okra (used for thickening) are the principal ingredients. Creole rice flecked with bits of red bell pepper and scallion is served with the gumbo, and chocolate praline *pôts de crème* are the finale.

In Menu 3, the cook offers a seafood stew that combines elements of a popular Creole pan-blackened (not burned) fish dish and the French seafood stew *bouillabaisse*. Asparagus vinaigrette and *jalapeño* biscuits go well with the flavorful entrée.

Beef grillades, here cubes of tenderloin braised in a seasoned sauce, served over garlicky cheese grits, make a delicious brunch or dinner. The crisp salad of chicory, pumpernickel croutons, and onion rings can be presented on the same plate or served separately.

Beef Grillades
Garlic-Cheese Grits
Chicory and Red Onion Salad with Pumpernickel Croutons

When dried and hulled corn kernels (hominy) are finely ground, the resultant particles are known as grits. In the South, grits are served in one form or another at almost every meal. Look for quick-cooking grits (which take only about 5 minutes to prepare) in any well-stocked supermarket, and store them in an airtight container, where they will keep indefinitely.

WHAT TO DRINK

A good beverage here would be dark beer, particularly stout. If you prefer wine, serve a simple red California Zinfandel, French Côtes du Rhône, or Italian Dolcetto.

SHOPPING LIST AND STAPLES

1½ pounds beef tenderloin tips, cut into ¾-inch cubes
Large head chicory
2 medium-size tomatoes (about 1 pound total weight)
Medium-size red onion
Medium-size yellow onion
Large bunch scallions
3 medium-size cloves garlic
Small bunch fresh thyme, or ½ teaspoon dried
½ cup milk
4 tablespoons unsalted butter
6 ounces sharp yellow Cheddar cheese
2 cups beef stock, preferably homemade (see page 10), or canned
¾ cup good-quality olive oil
2 tablespoons red wine vinegar
4 tablespoons Worcestershire sauce
2 tablespoons tomato paste
½ teaspoon hot pepper sauce
24-ounce box quick-cooking grits
1 loaf pumpernickel bread
1 cup all-purpose flour
1 bay leaf
Salt and freshly ground pepper

UTENSILS

Food processor (optional)
Medium-size heavy-gauge skillet
Large heavy-gauge saucepan
Medium-size heavy-gauge saucepan
Large bowl
Small bowl
Measuring cups and spoons
Chef's knife
Paring knife
2 wooden spoons
Slotted spoon
Grater (if not using food processor)

START-TO-FINISH STEPS

1. Peel and mince garlic for grillades and grits recipes. Peel onions. Slice red onion for salad recipe. Coarsely chop yellow onion for grillades recipe.
2. Follow grillades recipe steps 1 and 2 and salad recipe step 1.
3. Follow grillades recipe steps 3 through 6.
4. About fifteen minutes before grillades are done, follow grits recipe steps 1 and 2 and salad recipe steps 2 through 6.
5. Follow grits recipe steps 3 through 5, grillades recipe step 7, and serve with salad.

RECIPES

Beef Grillades

8 scallions
2 medium-size tomatoes (about 1 pound total weight)
Small bunch fresh thyme, or ½ teaspoon dried
2 cups beef stock
1 cup all-purpose flour
¼ cup good-quality olive oil
1½ pounds beef tenderloin tips, cut into ¾-inch cubes
Medium-size yellow onion, coarsely chopped
2 medium-size cloves garlic, minced
2 tablespoons tomato paste
4 tablespoons Worcestershire sauce
½ teaspoon hot pepper sauce
1 bay leaf
1 teaspoon freshly ground pepper
Salt
Garlic-Cheese Grits (see following recipe)

1. Wash and dry scallions, tomatoes, and fresh thyme if using. Mince 2 scallions and reserve for garnish. Coarsely chop remaining scallions. Core tomatoes and chop coarsely. Mince enough fresh thyme to measure 1½ teaspoons.
2. In medium-size saucepan, heat stock over low heat until hot.

58

3. Spread flour on sheet of waxed paper. Heat 2 tablespoons oil in large heavy-gauge saucepan over medium-high heat until almost smoking.

4. Dredge beef in flour and brown in oil 8 to 10 minutes. Using slotted spoon, transfer beef to plate.

5. Add remaining 2 tablespoons oil to large saucepan with fat from beef and heat until hot. Add chopped scallions, tomatoes, onion, and garlic and cook over medium heat 3 to 4 minutes, or until onion is translucent.

6. Return beef to saucepan and add hot stock, fresh or dried thyme, tomato paste, Worcestershire sauce, hot pepper sauce, bay leaf, pepper, and salt to taste. Stir to combine. Bring liquid to a simmer and cook beef over low heat 40 to 45 minutes, or until tender.

7. Discard bay leaf. Serve grillades over garlic-cheese grits and garnish with minced scallions.

Garlic-Cheese Grits

6 ounces sharp yellow Cheddar cheese
½ teaspoon salt
Medium-size clove garlic, minced
1 cup quick-cooking grits
4 tablespoons unsalted butter
½ cup milk

1. In food processor fitted with steel blade, or with grater, grate enough cheese to measure 1½ cups; set aside.

2. Bring 3 cups water and salt to a boil in medium-size heavy-gauge saucepan over medium-high heat.

3. Add garlic and slowly stir in grits. Return to a boil, reduce heat to low, and simmer 5 minutes, stirring constantly.

4. Cut butter into small pieces. Add butter, milk, and all but 2 tablespoons cheese to grits and stir until smooth.

5. Divide grits among 4 dinner plates and sprinkle with reserved cheese.

Chicory and Red Onion Salad with Pumpernickel Croutons

Large head chicory
½ cup good-quality olive oil
2 thick slices pumpernickel bread
2 tablespoons red wine vinegar
Salt and freshly ground pepper
Medium-size red onion, cut into ¼-inch-thick rings

1. Wash and dry chicory and tear into bite-size pieces; place in plastic bag and refrigerate until needed. Line plate with double thickness of paper towels.

2. In medium-size heavy-gauge skillet, heat 2 tablespoons oil over medium-high heat until hot.

3. Meanwhile, cut pumpernickel slices into 1-inch cubes.

4. Add bread cubes to oil and cook 2 to 3 minutes, or until evenly browned. Using slotted spoon, transfer croutons to paper-towel-lined plate to drain.

5. For dressing, combine remaining 6 tablespoons oil, vinegar, and salt and pepper to taste in small bowl, and beat with fork until combined.

6. In large bowl, combine chicory, onion rings, and croutons. Pour dressing over salad and toss to coat. Divide salad among 4 dinner plates.

ADDED TOUCH

Because crabmeat is delicate and can be ruined by overcooking, sauté the fritters quickly and remove them from the skillet promptly once they have browned.

Crab Fritters with Salsa

¾ pound fresh crabmeat, or two 6-ounce packages frozen, thawed
2 medium-size ripe tomatoes
1 each small red and green bell pepper
Small jalapeño chili
Small yellow onion
1 tablespoon unsalted butter
¼ cup all-purpose flour
1 teaspoon baking powder
¼ cup milk, approximately
2 eggs, lightly beaten
½ teaspoon Worcestershire sauce
½ teaspoon salt
¼ teaspoon hot pepper sauce
Dash of Cayenne pepper
¼ teaspoon freshly ground black pepper
¼ cup vegetable oil

1. Preheat oven to 200 degrees. Line heatproof platter with paper towels. Place crabmeat in large bowl. Carefully pick over crabmeat, discarding any cartilage or bits of shell. Flake crabmeat with fork and set aside.

2. Wash and dry tomatoes and bell peppers. Core and coarsely chop tomatoes. Core and seed peppers. Coarsely chop enough peppers to measure ¼ cup each. Finely chop enough remaining peppers to measure ¼ cup each; set aside. Wash and dry jalapeño chili. Wearing rubber gloves, seed, derib, and mince jalapeño.

3. Peel onion. Coarsely chop enough onion to measure ¼ cup and finely chop enough onion to measure ¼ cup; set aside.

4. For salsa, combine *coarsely* chopped vegetables and jalapeño in serving bowl; set aside.

5. In large heavy-gauge skillet, heat butter over medium heat until hot. Add *finely* chopped vegetables and sauté 2 minutes, or until soft.

6. Add sautéed vegetables to bowl with crabmeat. Add flour, baking powder, milk, eggs, Worcestershire sauce, salt, hot pepper sauce, Cayenne, and black pepper and mix well. (Add more milk if needed to make batter of dropping consistency.)

7. Heat oil in large heavy-gauge skillet over medium-high heat until hot. Add enough crab mixture by tablespoonsful to fit in skillet without crowding and cook 2 to 3 minutes on each side, or until browned. Remove fritters to paper-towel-lined platter and keep warm in oven. Repeat for remaining batter. You should have about 36 fritters.

8. Transfer fritters to serving platter. Serve with salsa.

Chicken and Okra Gumbo
Creole Rice
Chocolate Praline Pôts de Crème

Chicken and okra gumbo is served with a bowl of appetizing Creole rice and a rich dessert of chocolate praline pôts de crème.

The hearty gumbo contains okra, a popular southern vegetable brought to America by African slaves in the eighteenth century. A tapered green or white seed pod, okra exudes a thick liquid while cooking that gives substance to sauces. Buy tender pods that are no longer than 4 inches and that snap easily.

WHAT TO DRINK

The cook suggests serving a flavorful white wine, such as a Gewürztraminer, with this meal. Or try a Riesling from California, the Pacific Northwest, or Alsace.

SHOPPING LIST AND STAPLES

2½- to 3-pound chicken, cut into 8 pieces
¼ pound andouille sausage or kielbasa
1 each small green and red bell pepper
Small bunch celery
¼ pound fresh okra, or 10-ounce package frozen
Small yellow onion

Small bunch scallions
2 eggs
¾ cup milk
2 tablespoons unsalted butter
4 cups chicken stock, preferably homemade (see page 10), or canned
¼ cup vegetable oil
½ cup all-purpose flour
1 cup long-grain white rice
3-ounce can pecan halves
6-ounce package semi-sweet chocolate pieces
½ teaspoon instant coffee powder or espresso powder
½ teaspoon Cayenne pepper
1 bay leaf
Salt and freshly ground pepper
¼ cup hazelnut or praline liqueur

UTENSILS

Blender
Large heavy-gauge flameproof casserole with cover
Small heatproof casserole with cover

60

3 small saucepans
Large bowl
Medium-size metal bowl
Measuring cups and spoons
Chef's knife
Paring knife
2 wooden spoons
Metal tongs
Four 8-ounce ramekins or custard cups

START-TO-FINISH STEPS

One hour ahead: Set out frozen okra, if using, to thaw for gumbo recipe.

1. Wash, dry, core, and seed bell peppers. Coarsely chop enough green and red pepper for gumbo recipe. Mince enough red pepper for rice recipe.
2. Follow pôts de crème recipe step 1 and gumbo recipe step 1.
3. Follow rice recipe steps 1 through 3.
4. Follow pôts de crème recipe steps 2 through 6.
5. Follow rice recipe step 4.
6. While rice is cooking, follow gumbo recipe steps 2 through 7.
7. Follow rice recipe step 5 and gumbo recipe step 8.
8. Follow rice recipe step 6, gumbo recipe step 9, and serve.
9. Follow pôts de crème recipe step 7 and serve for dessert.

RECIPES

Chicken and Okra Gumbo

1 stalk celery
¼ pound fresh okra, or 10-ounce package frozen, thawed
Small yellow onion
½ cup all-purpose flour
½ teaspoon Cayenne pepper, approximately
Salt and freshly ground pepper
2½- to 3-pound chicken, cut into 8 pieces
2 cups chicken stock
¼ cup vegetable oil
1 tablespoon unsalted butter
½ cup each coarsely chopped green and red bell pepper
1 bay leaf
¼ pound andouille sausage or kielbasa

1. Wash celery, and fresh okra if using. Coarsely chop celery. Cut enough okra into 1-inch pieces to measure ½ cup; dice remaining okra to measure ¼ cup. Peel and coarsely chop onion.
2. In paper bag, combine flour, ½ teaspoon Cayenne, and salt and pepper to taste. Add chicken and shake to coat.
3. Heat stock in small saucepan over high heat until hot.
4. Meanwhile, line platter with paper towels; set aside. Heat oil in large heavy-gauge flameproof casserole over medium-high heat until very hot. Add chicken and cook, turning once, 5 to 7 minutes, or until well browned.

5. Using tongs, transfer chicken to paper-towel-lined platter to drain. Pour off oil from casserole and add butter, celery, 1-inch okra pieces, onion, and chopped bell peppers. Cook over medium-high heat, stirring, 3 to 5 minutes, or until okra is tender.
6. Return chicken to casserole and add hot stock and bay leaf. Partially cover pan. Bring gumbo to a simmer and cook over low heat 30 minutes.
7. Meanwhile, cut sausage into ¼-inch dice; set aside.
8. When gumbo has cooked 30 minutes, add sausage and season with salt, pepper, and additional Cayenne if desired. Simmer, uncovered, another 10 minutes.
9. Just before serving, discard bay leaf. Stir in diced okra and divide gumbo among 4 individual bowls.

Creole Rice

Medium-size scallion
2 cups chicken stock
1 cup long-grain white rice
2 tablespoons minced red bell pepper
1 tablespoon unsalted butter
1 teaspoon salt

1. Preheat oven to 375 degrees.
2. Wash and dry scallion and mince enough white and green parts to measure 2 tablespoons; set aside.
3. Heat stock in small saucepan over medium-high heat until hot.
4. Place scallion, hot stock, rice, bell pepper, butter, and salt in small heatproof casserole and stir to combine. Bake, covered, 40 to 45 minutes, or until rice is tender and stock is absorbed.
5. Turn off heat and keep rice warm in oven until ready to serve.
6. Divide rice among 4 individual bowls.

Chocolate Praline Pôts de Crème

¾ cup milk
⅓ cup pecan halves
1 cup semi-sweet chocolate pieces
2 eggs
½ teaspoon instant coffee powder or espresso powder
¼ cup hazelnut or praline liqueur

1. Place four 8-ounce ramekins or custard cups in freezer.
2. Scald milk over medium heat in small saucepan.
3. Meanwhile, reserving 4 pecan halves for garnish, place remaining pecans, chocolate, eggs, coffee powder, and liqueur in blender.
4. Add hot milk to blender and blend mixture at high speed 1 to 2 minutes, or until smooth.
5. Fill large bowl with ice cubes and 1 cup cold water. Pour milk mixture into medium-size metal bowl and place medium-size bowl in large bowl. Stir mixture 2 to 3 minutes, or until slightly cooled.
6. Pour mixture into chilled ramekins or custard cups and refrigerate at least 20 minutes, or until ready to serve.
7. Just before serving, garnish with pecan halves.

Blackened Seafood Stew
Asparagus Vinaigrette
Jalapeño Biscuits

Celebrate spring with a wholesome dinner of asparagus vinaigrette and Creole-style seafood stew. The homemade biscuits flecked with slivers of jalapeño should be kept warm in a napkin-lined basket.

The peak season for asparagus is April through late June; however, some fine greengrocers stock asparagus at other times of the year. Select plump, nicely rounded spears with compact tips.

WHAT TO DRINK

The seafood stew goes well with a crisp white wine, such as an Italian Verdicchio or a French Muscadet.

SHOPPING LIST AND STAPLES

2 pounds firm-fleshed fish fillets, such as salmon, halibut, or swordfish, or any combination
16 medium-size fresh shrimp, shelled and deveined, or 16 oysters or clams
1 pound asparagus
Small bunch celery
Medium-size green bell pepper
2 ears fresh corn, or 10-ounce package frozen kernels
2 medium-size tomatoes
Small jalapeño chili
Medium-size yellow onion
Small bunch fresh dill, or 2 teaspoons dried
1 cup milk
2 tablespoons unsalted butter
2½ cups fish stock, preferably homemade (see page 10), or three 8-ounce bottles clam juice
2-ounce jar imported capers
½ cup good-quality olive oil
2 tablespoons vegetable oil
2 tablespoons red wine vinegar
1 teaspoon Dijon mustard
5 tablespoons vegetable shortening
2 cups unbleached flour
1 tablespoon baking powder
½ teaspoon Cayenne pepper
Salt and freshly ground black pepper

UTENSILS

Large cast-iron skillet
Large saucepan with cover
Large flameproof casserole
17 x 11-inch baking sheet
Large bowl
Small nonaluminum bowl

Colander
Small strainer
Measuring cups and spoons
Chef's knife
Paring knife
Metal spatula
Metal tongs
Flour sifter or sieve
Rolling pin
2½- or 3-inch round biscuit cutter
Stiff-bristled brush

START-TO-FINISH STEPS

One hour ahead: Set out frozen corn, if using, to thaw.

1. Prepare bell pepper and jalapeño.
2. Follow asparagus recipe step 1 and stew recipe steps 1 through 3.
3. Follow biscuits recipe step 1 and asparagus recipe steps 2 through 6.
4. Follow stew recipe steps 4 through 6.
5. Follow biscuits recipe steps 2 through 6.
6. While biscuits bake, follow stew recipe steps 7 and 8 and asparagus recipe step 7.
7. Follow biscuits recipe step 7, stew recipe step 9, and serve with asparagus.

RECIPES

Blackened Seafood Stew

16 medium-size fresh shrimp, shelled and deveined, or 16 oysters or clams
1 stalk celery
2 medium-size tomatoes
Small bunch fresh dill, or 2 teaspoons dried
2 ears fresh corn, or 10-ounce package frozen corn kernels, thawed
Medium-size yellow onion
2 tablespoons unsalted butter
Medium-size green bell pepper, coarsely chopped
2 tablespoons vegetable oil
2 pounds firm-fleshed fish fillets
½ teaspoon Cayenne pepper
Salt and freshly ground black pepper
2½ cups fish stock or clam juice

1. If using oysters or clams, scrub and rinse thoroughly.
2. Wash and dry celery, tomatoes, and fresh dill if using. Cut celery diagonally into ½-inch-thick slices. Core tomatoes and cut into 8 wedges. Chop enough dill to measure 2 tablespoons plus 1 teaspoon.
3. Shuck fresh corn, if using. With chef's knife, cut off kernels. Peel and coarsely chop onion.
4. Heat butter in large flameproof casserole over medium-high heat until foam subsides. Add celery, onion, and green pepper and cook 10 to 12 minutes, or until tender.
5. Meanwhile, heat oil in large cast-iron skillet over high heat until smoking.
6. Sprinkle fish fillets on both sides with Cayenne, salt, and black pepper. Sear fish in skillet 2 minutes on each side, or until dark golden brown. Using metal spatula, transfer fish to large plate. If using shrimp, sear 1 minute on each side. Transfer shrimp to small plate.
7. Add stock, tomatoes, and fresh or frozen corn to vegetables in casserole, reduce heat, and simmer 5 minutes.
8. Cut seared fish into 2-inch pieces and add to casserole with 2 tablespoons fresh dill or all of dried dill. Add shrimp, oysters, or clams. Simmer 4 to 5 minutes, or until fish is firm and oysters or clams have opened.
9. Sprinkle stew with remaining fresh dill, if using, and serve.

Asparagus Vinaigrette

1 pound asparagus
1 teaspoon capers
½ cup good-quality olive oil
2 tablespoons red wine vinegar
1 teaspoon Dijon mustard
Salt and freshly ground pepper

1. Bring 3 quarts water to a boil in large saucepan over high heat.
2. Trim asparagus. Peel stalks, if desired, and rinse.
3. Drain capers in small strainer.
4. Combine capers, oil, vinegar, and mustard in small nonaluminum bowl; beat with fork until well blended.
5. Add asparagus to boiling water. Simmer, covered, 3 to 5 minutes, or until asparagus is tender.
6. Using tongs, gently transfer asparagus to colander and refresh under cold running water. Set aside to drain.
7. To serve, arrange asparagus on serving platter. Beat dressing to recombine and pour over asparagus. Sprinkle with salt and pepper to taste, and serve.

Jalapeño Biscuits

2 cups unbleached flour
1 tablespoon baking powder
1 teaspoon salt
5 tablespoons vegetable shortening
1 cup milk
1 tablespoon thinly sliced jalapeño chili

1. Preheat oven to 400 degrees.
2. Sift together flour, baking powder, and salt into large bowl. Add shortening and blend mixture with 2 knives until it resembles coarse cornmeal.
3. Add milk and jalapeño and mix with fork until mixture forms a dough.
4. Gather dough into a ball and knead on lightly floured surface 1 minute.
5. Roll out dough to ½-inch thickness. With floured 2½- or 3-inch round cutter, cut out biscuits.
6. Place biscuits on ungreased 17 x 11-inch baking sheet and bake 12 to 15 minutes, or until golden brown.
7. Transfer biscuits to napkin-lined basket and serve.

David Ricketts

D avid Ricketts describes the meals he prepares as survival cooking. "I work long hours, so I do not have time to fuss," he says. "Whatever I cook—whether it is for myself or for company—must take only minimal preparation time." He relies on his well-stocked cupboards to provide the basics for a meal, then fills in with a quick trip to local markets.

When he plans a menu, he often lets one of the main ingredients inspire the theme. For instance, tortellini—the foundation for the robust soup with creamy hot pepper sauce in Menu 1—gives this dinner an Italian feeling. With the piquant soup, he offers sautéed spinach and cucumber crescents and, for dessert, fresh fruit with chopped pistachios.

Menu 2 is a southern supper featuring sweet yams and ham. These two ingredients—staples in the American South—are combined in an unusual main-course soup flavored with fresh ginger, orange zest, apple juice, and bourbon if desired. Pungent tarragon-mustard popovers and a summer-squash salad served in radicchio cups complete the meal.

In Menu 3, David Ricketts prepares a hearty repast that might well be served in Minnesota, where most of America's wild rice is grown. Here the wild rice is featured in a thick soup that also contains vegetables and kielbasa sausage. The fennel and red pepper salad can be served with the meal or as an appetizer.

A tomato-tinted tortellini soup topped with a spoonful of creamy hot pepper sauce is an easy main course. Sautéed spinach and cucumber crescents and fresh fruit sprinkled with pistachios are the perfect complements. Sesame bread sticks are an optional addition.

Tortellini Soup with Creamy Hot Pepper Sauce
Sautéed Spinach and Cucumber
Mixed Fruit Salad with Pistachios

The focal point of this vegetarian meal is a tortellini soup topped with a sauce that is a variation on the Provençal garlic mayonnaise *rouille*. Here the sauce contains Cayenne pepper and red pepper flakes to give it bite. Let guests add as much of the spicy sauce as they like.

Tortellini are small, stuffed ring-shaped pasta sometimes called "navels of Venus." Here the cook uses tortellini filled with cheese. You can readily find frozen or dried tortellini in many supermarkets.

WHAT TO DRINK

Choose a somewhat acidic wine with plenty of character for this meal. For white, try a California Sauvignon Blanc or an Italian Verdicchio. For red, select a young Chianti—preferably one from the Classico zone.

SHOPPING LIST AND STAPLES

2 large bunches spinach (about 2 pounds total weight)
2 medium-size carrots (about 6 ounces total weight)
Large cucumber (about 10 ounces)
Small yellow onion
3 medium-size cloves garlic
Small bunch mint
Small bunch flat-leaf parsley
Large honeydew melon
Large ripe papaya
2 large ripe pears (about ¾ pound total weight)
Small lemon
3 eggs
½ pint heavy cream
4 tablespoons unsalted butter
1 pound frozen or dried cheese tortellini
14-ounce can peeled Italian plum tomatoes
16-ounce can tomato purée
4-ounce jar roasted red peppers
1 cup plus 3 tablespoons good-quality olive oil
1 tablespoon balsamic vinegar
2¼-ounce package shelled pistachio nuts
½ teaspoon crushed red pepper flakes
½ teaspoon Cayenne pepper
Salt and freshly ground black pepper
¼ cup Cointreau, Triple Sec, or other orange-flavored liqueur

UTENSILS

Food processor or blender
Large heavy-gauge nonaluminum saucepan or flameproof casserole, with cover
Large heavy-gauge nonaluminum skillet with cover
Large nonaluminum bowl
2 small bowls
Colander
Measuring cups and spoons
Chef's knife
Paring knife
Wooden spoon
Rubber spatula
Vegetable peeler
Ladle

START-TO-FINISH STEPS

1. Follow fruit salad recipe steps 1 through 5.
2. Follow hot pepper sauce recipe steps 1 through 4.
3. Follow spinach and cucumber recipe steps 1 through 3.
4. While spinach cooks, follow soup recipe steps 1 through 4.
5. Follow spinach and cucumber recipe step 4, soup recipe steps 5 and 6, and fruit salad recipe step 6.
6. Follow soup recipe step 7 and spinach recipe step 5.
7. Follow soup recipe step 8, spinach recipe step 6, and serve.
8. Follow fruit salad recipe step 7 and serve for dessert.

RECIPES

Tortellini Soup with Creamy Hot Pepper Sauce

Small yellow onion
2 medium-size carrots (about 6 ounces total weight)
2 tablespoons good-quality olive oil
14-ounce can peeled Italian plum tomatoes
1 cup tomato purée
1 pound frozen or dried cheese tortellini
Small bunch flat-leaf parsley
½ cup heavy cream
Salt and freshly ground black pepper
Creamy Hot Pepper Sauce (see following recipe)

1. Halve and peel onion. Peel and trim carrots.
2. Using food processor fitted with steel blade, or chef's knife, coarsely chop onion and carrots.

66

3. Heat oil in large heavy-gauge nonaluminum saucepan or flameproof casserole over medium heat. Add onion and carrots and sauté about 3 minutes, or until slightly softened.

4. Stir in tomatoes with their juice, breaking up tomatoes with wooden spoon. Stir in tomato purée and 3 cups water. Cover, increase heat to high, and bring to a boil.

5. Add tortellini and reduce heat to low. Cover and simmer 10 to 12 minutes, according to package directions, or until tortellini are tender.

6. While tortellini cook, wash and dry parsley. Finely chop enough parsley to measure 1 teaspoon. Reserve remaining parsley for another use.

7. Add heavy cream to saucepan or casserole and stir to blend. Season soup very lightly with salt and freshly ground black pepper. Keep warm over very low heat until ready to serve.

8. To serve, ladle soup into 4 large bowls. Top each with a spoonful of creamy hot pepper sauce and ¼ teaspoon chopped parsley. Serve extra sauce on the side.

Creamy Hot Pepper Sauce

2 or 3 medium-size cloves garlic
4-ounce jar roasted red peppers
Small lemon
3 eggs
½ teaspoon Cayenne pepper
½ teaspoon crushed red pepper flakes
1 cup good-quality olive oil
Salt

1. Crush and peel garlic. Drain roasted peppers and set aside enough to measure ¼ cup. Halve lemon and squeeze enough juice to measure 1 tablespoon. Separate eggs, placing yolks in small bowl and reserving whites for another use.

2. In food processor fitted with steel blade, or in blender, combine garlic, roasted peppers, lemon juice, egg yolks, Cayenne, and red pepper flakes.

3. With motor running, add oil in a thin, steady stream, stopping frequently to scrape down sides of container with rubber spatula. Add salt to taste.

4. Scrape sauce into small bowl. Cover tightly with plastic wrap and set aside until needed.

Sautéed Spinach and Cucumber

2 large bunches spinach (about 2 pounds total weight)
Large cucumber (about 10 ounces)
4 tablespoons unsalted butter
1 tablespoon good-quality olive oil
1 tablespoon balsamic vinegar
Salt and freshly ground black pepper

1. Remove tough stems from spinach and discard any blemished leaves. Wash spinach in several changes of cold water. Do not dry.

2. Peel cucumber and halve lengthwise. Using teaspoon,

remove and discard seeds. (See illustration below.) Cut cucumber halves crosswise into ⅛-inch-thick slices; set aside.

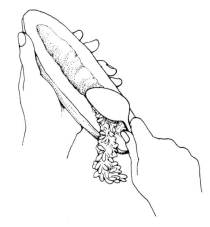

3. Place damp spinach in large heavy-gauge nonaluminum skillet. Cover and cook over medium heat, stirring occasionally, 5 to 10 minutes, or just until wilted.

4. Drain spinach in colander, but do not squeeze leaves.

5. Heat butter and oil in same large nonaluminum skillet over medium heat until butter melts. Add drained spinach and cucumber slices and sauté 3 to 4 minutes, or just until heated through. Sprinkle with vinegar, and season with salt and pepper to taste.

6. Divide sautéed spinach and cucumber among 4 salad plates and serve.

Mixed Fruit Salad with Pistachios

⅓ cup shelled pistachio nuts
Large honeydew melon
Large ripe papaya
2 large ripe pears (about ¾ pound total weight)
¼ cup Cointreau, Triple Sec, or other orange-flavored liqueur
Small bunch mint

1. Coarsely chop pistachios; set aside.

2. Halve honeydew and remove and discard seeds. Cut one half of honeydew in two; set aside one quarter and reserve remaining quarter and half for another use. Trim rind from quarter and cut quarter into 1½-inch chunks. Place honeydew in large nonaluminum bowl.

3. Peel and halve papaya. Remove and discard seeds. Cut flesh into 1½-inch chunks and place in bowl with honeydew.

4. Wash and dry pears. Halve pears lengthwise and remove stems and cores. Cut into 1½-inch chunks and add to bowl with other fruit.

5. Sprinkle pistachios and liqueur over fruit and toss to coat. Cover and refrigerate until ready to serve.

6. Wash and dry mint. Set aside 4 large sprigs for garnish; reserve remaining mint for another use.

7. To serve, divide fruit among 4 shallow plates and garnish each serving with a mint sprig.

Yam and Ham Soup with Ginger
Tarragon-Mustard Popovers
Shredded Squash and Carrot Salad

Down-home flavors mingle with the exotic in the yam, ham, and ginger soup served with popovers and a summer-squash salad.

Unlike other quick breads, popovers require no leavening to make them rise. They achieve their puffiness from the high proportion of liquid in the batter, which is converted to steam as the popovers bake in the hot oven. To get the most expansion, stir the batter just until it has the consistency of heavy cream, and use a popover pan or a muffin pan that has cups that are deeper than they are wide so the batter can expand only upward. Because popovers are fragile and can collapse if exposed to a sudden draft, do not open the oven door to peek at them until they are finished baking. Time the popovers carefully so they come hot from the oven as the meal begins.

WHAT TO DRINK

A white wine with a hint of spice is called for here. The cook suggests a dry Alsatian Riesling for a subtle complement; an Alsatian Gewürztraminer would make a more assertive partner. Or try a Riesling or Gewürztraminer from California or the Pacific Northwest.

SHOPPING LIST AND STAPLES

¾ pound baked ham, in one piece
3 or 4 medium-size yams (about 2 pounds total weight)

3 small zucchini (about ¾ pound total weight)
Small yellow squash
Large head radicchio
3 large carrots (about ¾ pound total weight)
Medium-size onion
1-inch piece fresh ginger
Small bunch parsley
Medium-size orange
Large lemon
2 eggs
1 cup milk
2 tablespoons unsalted butter
2 tablespoons lightly salted butter
2½ cups chicken stock, preferably homemade (see page 10), or canned
½ pint apple juice
¼ cup plus 1 tablespoon vegetable oil
3 tablespoons Dijon mustard
1 cup all-purpose flour
2 teaspoons dried tarragon
Salt and freshly ground black pepper
2 tablespoons bourbon (optional)

UTENSILS

Food processor or blender
Large heavy-gauge saucepan or flameproof casserole, with cover
Small saucepan
8-cup heavy-gauge popover pan or 12-cup muffin pan
Large nonaluminum bowl
Medium-size bowl
2 small bowls, 1 nonaluminum
Measuring cups and spoons
Chef's knife
Paring knife
2 wooden spoons
Slotted spoon
Rubber spatula
Grater
Whisk
Pastry brush
Flour sifter or sieve
Vegetable peeler
Ladle

START-TO-FINISH STEPS

Thirty minutes ahead: Set out eggs to come to room temperature for popovers recipe.

1. Follow popovers recipe steps 1 and 2.
2. Follow soup recipe steps 1 through 6.
3. While yams cook, follow popovers recipe steps 3 through 5.
4. While popovers bake, follow soup recipe steps 7 and 8.
5. Follow popovers recipe step 6.

6. While popovers continue to bake, follow salad recipe steps 1 through 5.
7. Follow soup recipe step 9, popovers recipe step 7, and serve with salad.

RECIPES

Yam and Ham Soup with Ginger

Medium-size onion
2 large carrots (about ½ pound total weight)
1-inch piece fresh ginger
Medium-size orange
2 tablespoons unsalted butter
1 tablespoon vegetable oil
2½ cups chicken stock
1 cup apple juice
Small bunch parsley
3 or 4 medium-size yams (about 2 pounds total weight)
¾ pound baked ham, in one piece
2 tablespoons bourbon (optional)
Salt
Freshly ground black pepper

1. Halve and peel onion. Peel and trim carrots. Using paring knife or vegetable peeler, peel ginger. In food processor fitted with steel blade, or with chef's knife, coarsely chop onion, carrots, and ginger; set aside.
2. Wash orange and dry with paper towels. Using grater, finely grate enough zest to measure 6 teaspoons; set aside.
3. In large heavy-gauge saucepan or flameproof casserole, melt butter with oil over medium heat. Add chopped vegetables and 2 teaspoons grated orange zest and reduce heat to low. Cover pan and cook vegetables, stirring occasionally, 3 to 5 minutes, or until softened.
4. Stir in chicken stock and apple juice. Cover pan, increase heat to high, and bring liquid to a boil.
5. Meanwhile, wash and dry parsley. Finely chop enough parsley to measure 2 teaspoons; set aside. Pare yams with vegetable peeler and cut enough into small dice to measure about 6 cups.
6. Add yams to boiling stock and reduce heat to medium. Gently boil yams, partially covered, 5 to 10 minutes, or until tender.
7. Cut enough ham into ¼-inch dice to measure about 2 cups; set aside.
8. Using slotted spoon, transfer 3 cups cooked yams to food processor or blender. Process, adding a little of the soup liquid, until yams become a smooth purée. Using rubber spatula, scrape purée back into soup and stir to blend. Add ham, and bourbon if using. Simmer gently until ham is heated through. Add salt and pepper to taste and keep soup warm over very low heat until ready to serve.
9. To serve, ladle soup into 4 individual bowls. Garnish each serving with ½ teaspoon chopped parsley and 1 teaspoon orange zest.

Tarragon-Mustard Popovers

1 cup all-purpose flour
2 eggs, at room temperature
2 tablespoons lightly salted butter
1 cup milk
1 to 3 tablespoons Dijon mustard
2 teaspoons dried tarragon, crumbled

1. Preheat oven to 450 degrees. Sift flour onto sheet of waxed paper; measure 1 cup flour and set aside. Break eggs into small bowl and beat lightly; set aside.
2. Melt butter in small saucepan over medium heat. Transfer 1 tablespoon melted butter to medium-size bowl; set aside. Lightly brush insides of popover pan cups, or 10 muffin pan cups, with remaining melted butter.
3. Add milk, mustard to taste, tarragon, and eggs to bowl with melted butter. Add flour and stir just until blended; do *not* overmix. Batter should be the consistency of heavy cream.
4. Ladle batter into prepared cups, filling each about two-thirds full. Fill any empty cups with water to prevent scorching.
5. Place pan in oven and bake popovers 15 minutes.
6. Reduce oven temperature to 350 degrees and bake popovers another 15 minutes, or until golden; do not open oven door.
7. Remove pan from oven. Turn out popovers and serve immediately.

Shredded Squash and Carrot Salad

Large head radicchio
3 small zucchini (about ¾ pound total weight)
Small yellow squash
Large carrot
Large lemon
¼ cup vegetable oil
Salt and freshly ground black pepper

1. Wash and dry radicchio and separate leaves. Discard any bruised or discolored leaves. Wash and dry zucchini, yellow squash, and carrot; trim ends. Peel carrot. Halve lemon and squeeze enough juice to measure ¼ cup.
2. Place grater in large nonaluminum bowl and coarsely shred zucchini, squash, and carrot. Gently toss to combine.
3. For dressing, in small nonaluminum bowl, whisk together lemon juice, oil, and salt and pepper to taste.

4. Pour dressing over grated vegetables and mix gently.
5. Using 3 radicchio leaves for each, form cups on 4 plates. Divide shredded vegetables among radicchio cups.

ADDED TOUCH

This European-style bittersweet chocolate sauce for ice cream can be put together at the last minute, or be prepared up to 3 days in advance, and then refrigerated. To reheat, place the sauce in the top of a double boiler over gently simmering water. The broiled sugar will keep indefinitely in a covered container.

Vanilla Ice Cream with Chocolate "Praline" Sauce

4-ounce can pecan pieces
4 squares (4 ounces) semisweet chocolate
2 squares (2 ounces) unsweetened chocolate
1 teaspoon powdered instant espresso
½ cup heavy cream
4 tablespoons unsalted butter
1 to 2 tablespoons Cognac or other brandy
1 cup firmly packed brown sugar
1 quart good-quality vanilla ice cream

1. Preheat oven to 450 degrees.
2. Spread pecans on medium-size cookie sheet. Toast in oven, stirring frequently, about 5 minutes, or until medium brown. Remove from oven and set aside to cool slightly.
3. Turn oven to broil.
4. Melt chocolate in top of double boiler over simmering water or in heavy-bottomed saucepan over very low heat.
5. Add espresso powder and cream and stir with wooden spoon until well blended. Remove pan from heat.
6. Cut butter into small pieces. Add to sauce and stir until well blended. Stir in brandy and pecan pieces.
7. Lightly grease medium-size cookie sheet. Force brown sugar through strainer onto baking sheet to form ¼-inch-thick layer. Place baking sheet under broiler, 4 inches from heat, about 15 seconds, watching closely to prevent sugar from burning, until sugar almost melts. Transfer cookie sheet to wire rack to cool.
8. When cool, lift sugar from baking sheet with metal spatula and break into small pieces.
9. Spoon chocolate sauce over vanilla ice cream. Garnish with brown sugar pieces.

Wild Rice Soup with Sausage
Fennel and Red Pepper Salad
Orange Gingersnaps

Wild rice and sausage soup with fennel salad and bread will take the chill off a fall evening. Spicy gingersnaps are the finale.

A distinctive fennel salad with roasted red peppers counters the richness of the wild rice soup. Fennel is a popular Italian vegetable, also known as *finocchio*, Florence fennel, or anise. It is generally available in supermarkets in fall and winter. Try to find short, squat fennel bulbs, which are crisper and sweeter than the elongated variety. Always select firm fennel bulbs with creamy greenish-white stalks. Slice the fennel as thinly as possible.

WHAT TO DRINK

This flavorful soup goes well with a dry, fruity red wine. There are many options: from California, a young Zinfandel or Gamay Beaujolais; from France, a Beaujolais from a village such as Fleurie, Juliénas, or Chiroubles; from Italy, a Dolcetto or young Chianti; or from Spain, a young Rioja.

SHOPPING LIST AND STAPLES

¾ pound kielbasa or other cooked smoked sausage
2 or 3 small fennel bulbs (1½ to 2½ pounds total weight)
Small bunch celery
2 large carrots (about ½ pound total weight)
Medium-size onion
Small bunch parsley
Large orange
1 egg
1 stick plus 4 tablespoons unsalted butter
5 to 6 cups chicken stock, preferably homemade (see page 10), or canned
4-ounce jar roasted red peppers
1 tablespoon vegetable oil
3 tablespoons good-quality olive oil
1 tablespoon white wine vinegar
¼ cup molasses
2 cups all-purpose flour
1 cup sugar
¾ teaspoon baking soda
4-ounce package wild rice
8-ounce package dried apricots (optional)
2 teaspoons ground ginger
Salt
Freshly ground pepper
2 tablespoons orange-flavored liqueur

UTENSILS

Food processor (optional)
Electric mixer
Large heavy-gauge saucepan or flameproof casserole, with cover
Two 17 x 11-inch cookie sheets
Medium-size bowl
2 small bowls, 1 nonaluminum
Large strainer
Measuring cups and spoons
Chef's knife
Paring knife
Wooden spoon
Metal spatula
Rubber spatula
Grater or zester
Ladle
Flour sifter or sieve
Wire cooling rack
Vegetable peeler

START-TO-FINISH STEPS

Thirty minutes ahead: Set out eggs and 1 stick butter to come to room temperature for cookie recipe.

1. Follow soup recipe steps 1 through 7.
2. While rice cooks, follow cookie recipe steps 1 through 8.
3. While first batch of cookies is baking, follow salad recipe steps 1 through 3.
4. Follow cookie recipe steps 9 and 10.
5. While second batch of cookies is baking, follow soup recipe step 8 and salad recipe step 4.
6. Follow cookie recipe step 11.
7. Follow soup recipe step 9 and serve with salad.
8. Serve cookies for dessert.

RECIPES

Wild Rice Soup with Sausage

Medium-size onion
2 large carrots (about ½ pound total weight)
2 large stalks celery (about 6 ounces total weight)
4 tablespoons unsalted butter
1 tablespoon vegetable oil
⅔ cup wild rice

5 to 6 cups chicken stock
¾ pound kielbasa or other cooked smoked sausage
2 dried apricot halves for garnish (optional)
Small bunch parsley

1. Halve and peel onion. Peel and trim carrots. Wash, dry, and trim celery. Using chef's knife, or in food processor fitted with steel blade, coarsely chop onion, carrots, and celery.
2. Heat butter and oil in large heavy-gauge saucepan or flameproof casserole over medium-high heat until butter melts.
3. Add onion, carrots, and celery to pan. Cover and cook over medium heat 3 to 5 minutes, or until vegetables are softened.
4. Meanwhile, place rice in large strainer and rinse thoroughly under cold running water.
5. Combine wild rice with vegetables, cover, and cook 2 minutes.
6. Add 5 cups stock, increase heat to high, and bring to a boil. Reduce heat and simmer 35 to 40 minutes, or until rice is firm but tender, adding more stock if necessary.
7. Meanwhile, cut kielbasa into thin slices. Stack 3 or 4 slices and cut into thin matchsticks. Cut dried apricot halves, if using, into thin strips; set aside. Wash and dry parsley. Set aside 4 sprigs for garnish.
8. When rice is almost done, stir kielbasa into soup. Reduce heat to very low and keep warm until ready to serve.
9. To serve, ladle soup into 4 soup bowls. Garnish each with a parsley sprig, and some apricot strips if using.

Fennel and Red Pepper Salad

2 or 3 small fennel bulbs (1½ to 2½ pounds total
  weight)
4-ounce jar roasted red peppers
3 tablespoons good-quality olive oil
1 tablespoon white wine vinegar
Salt
Freshly ground pepper

1. Trim stalks and root ends from fennel bulbs, reserving feathery tops for garnish. Wash fennel tops and bulbs and dry with paper towels. Slice fennel bulbs crosswise as thinly as possible. Drain red peppers and cut into thin strips.
2. Arrange fennel slices on 4 plates. Arrange red pepper strips over fennel.

3. For dressing, in small nonaluminum bowl, combine olive oil, vinegar, and salt and pepper to taste and beat with fork; set aside.
4. When ready to serve, drizzle each salad with dressing and garnish with reserved fennel tops.

Orange Gingersnaps

Large orange
1 stick unsalted butter, at room temperature
1 cup sugar
1 egg, at room temperature
¼ cup molasses
2 tablespoons orange-flavored liqueur
2 cups all-purpose flour
2 teaspoons ground ginger
¾ teaspoon baking soda

1. Preheat oven to 325 degrees.
2. Finely grate enough orange zest to measure 2 tablespoons; set aside. Reserve orange for another use.
3. Beat butter in medium-size bowl with electric mixer on medium speed until light. Gradually beat in sugar until light and fluffy, scraping down sides of bowl with rubber spatula as necessary.
4. In small bowl, lightly beat egg. Add egg, molasses, orange zest, and liqueur to butter-sugar mixture and beat on medium speed until well blended.
5. Sift together flour, ginger, and baking soda onto sheet of waxed paper. Gradually add to dough and beat on low speed until well blended.
6. Lightly butter two 17 x 11-inch cookie sheets. Divide dough in half, then divide one half into 10 equal pieces.
7. Roll each piece of dough between palms of hands to form a 1¼-inch ball. Arrange balls 3 inches apart on cookie sheet. Cover remaining dough with plastic wrap and refrigerate until needed.
8. Bake cookies 15 minutes, or until medium brown and slightly puffed with a crinkly top.
9. Five minutes before first batch is done, roll remaining dough into ten 1¼-inch balls and arrange on second cookie sheet.
10. Remove first batch of cookies from oven and place second batch in oven. With metal spatula, remove first batch of cookies from cookie sheet, transfer to wire rack and allow to cool.
11. Remove second batch of cookies from oven and let cool on wire rack.

Charlotte Walker

Having grown up in the Southwest, Charlotte Walker favors the bold flavors and colors of southwestern and Mexican food. The three soup and stew menus she presents here are all Tex-Mex. The striking *sopa seca* ("dry soup") of Menu 1 is a dish she often serves to company. In Mexico, this pasta-based dish is usually served following a "wet" soup and before the main course. Here it *is* the entrée, with chicken breasts and vegetables added to supplement the pasta. The accompanying *Cinco de Mayo* salad is named for a Mexican holiday (the fifth of May) and is arranged to resemble the Mexican flag, with rows of green, white, and red vegetables. Although this meal may take you a full hour to prepare, it is well worth the effort.

Menus 2 and 3 are quicker to put together, and both feature beans in the main course. In Menu 2, the cook serves steaming bowls of meatless three-bean chili sparked with cumin and hot *salsa*. The garnishes of sour cream, scallions, olives, coriander, and cheese turn what might be a plain dish into a real eye-stopper.

In Menu 3, Charlotte Walker offers black bean soup, made colorful by the addition of tomatoes and ham. This thick soup, served with warmed flour tortillas, avocado butter, and a lime- and tequila-based cream pudding for dessert, will surely please a hungry gathering.

These festive dishes are an ideal buffet brunch or supper. Start with endive leaves topped with guacamole and shrimp, then bring on the Mexican sopa seca *in a large earthenware bowl. The vegetable salad features tomatoes, jícama, and zucchini.*

75

Endive with Guacamole and Shrimp
Sopa Seca
Cinco de Mayo Salad

This substantial meal begins with an appetizer of guacamole and shrimp on crisp leaves of Belgian endive. For the guacamole, you will need a ripe avocado. If you cannot find one, ripen the fruit at home by putting it into a paper bag and leaving it at room temperature for a day or two. To speed the process, place a ripe tomato or banana in the bag with the avocado. To test for ripeness, stick a toothpick into the stem end of the avocado. If it slides in and out easily, the avocado is ready to use. A ripe avocado, stored in the refrigerator, will keep for 3 to 5 days.

Jícama is a component of the tricolored salad. This crunchy tuber looks like a brown-skinned turnip and tastes like a cross between an apple and a water chestnut. You can find whole or cut-up jícama in well-stocked supermarkets and Latin American groceries. Refrigerate the whole tuber in a plastic bag; keep cut-up jícama immersed in water in a covered container. If jícama is unavailable, use turnip instead.

WHAT TO DRINK

The bright flavors of this menu go well with just about any beverage, from mineral water to wine. The best choice for wine would be a reasonably full-bodied white, such as a Pinot Blanc from California, Italy, or Alsace.

SHOPPING LIST AND STAPLES

2 boneless, skinless chicken breast halves (about ¾ pound total weight)
36 cooked and peeled baby shrimp
3 small tomatoes (about ¾ pound total weight)
1 pint cherry tomatoes
Small head romaine lettuce
2 small heads Belgian endive (6 to 8 ounces total weight)
Large green bell pepper
Medium-size zucchini
⅓ pound jícama
Medium-size onion
2 large cloves garlic
Small bunch fresh coriander
Small bunch fresh oregano, or ½ teaspoon dried
Large ripe avocado (8 to 10 ounces), preferably Hass variety
Small lime

2 ounces Parmesan or Romano cheese, preferably imported
4 cups chicken stock, preferably homemade (see page 10), or canned
½ cup good-quality olive oil
3 tablespoons vegetable oil
3 tablespoons white wine vinegar
1 tablespoon Dijon mustard
1 tablespoon mayonnaise
¾ pound vermicelli
1 teaspoon ground cumin
⅜ teaspoon Cayenne pepper, approximately
Salt

UTENSILS

Food processor (optional)
Large heavy-gauge sauté pan with cover
Medium-size saucepan
Medium-size nonaluminum bowl
2 small nonaluminum bowls
Salad spinner (optional)
Measuring cups and spoons
Chef's knife
Paring knife
Wooden spoon
Slotted spoon
Grater (if not using food processor)
Citrus juicer (optional)
Whisk
Vegetable peeler

START-TO-FINISH STEPS

1. Wash and dry coriander. Reserve 10 sprigs for endive recipe and 2 sprigs for salad recipe, if using, and mince enough remaining coriander to measure 1 teaspoon for sopa seca recipe.
2. Follow endive recipe steps 1 through 4.
3. Follow sopa seca recipe steps 1 through 6.
4. While chicken poaches, follow salad recipe steps 1 through 4.
5. Follow sopa seca recipe steps 7 and 8 and serve endive as first course.
6. Follow sopa seca recipe steps 9 though 11 and salad recipe step 5.
7. Follow sopa seca recipe step 12 and serve with salad.

RECIPES

Endive with Guacamole and Shrimp

2 small heads Belgian endive (6 to 8 ounces total weight)
Large ripe avocado (8 to 10 ounces), preferably Hass variety
Small lime
1 tablespoon mayonnaise
⅛ teaspoon Cayenne pepper, approximately
Salt
36 cooked and peeled baby shrimp
10 sprigs coriander for garnish (optional)

1. Trim stem ends of endive and separate leaves. Wash leaves and dry in salad spinner or with paper towels. Place 12 of the largest leaves on serving platter; reserve remaining endive for another use.
2. Halve avocado lengthwise and discard pit. Using small spoon, scoop out pulp into small nonaluminum bowl. Halve lime and squeeze enough juice to measure 1 teaspoon.
3. Mash avocado with fork. Stir in lime juice and mayonnaise. Season with Cayenne and salt to taste.
4. Place a spoonful of guacamole in center of each endive leaf and top with 3 shrimp. Garnish platter with coriander sprigs, if desired. Cover and refrigerate until ready to serve.

Sopa Seca

4 cups chicken stock
3 small tomatoes (about ¾ pound total weight)
Large green bell pepper
Medium-size onion
2 large cloves garlic
2 ounces Parmesan or Romano cheese, preferably imported
2 boneless, skinless chicken breast halves (about ¾ pound total weight)
3 tablespoons vegetable oil
¾ pound vermicelli
1 teaspoon ground cumin
¼ teaspoon Cayenne pepper
Salt
1 teaspoon minced coriander for garnish

1. Bring stock to a boil in medium-size saucepan over medium-high heat.
2. Wash, dry, core, and coarsely chop tomatoes.
3. Wash and dry green bell pepper. Core, seed, and dice pepper.
4. Halve, peel, and finely chop onion. Crush, peel, and mince garlic.
5. Using food processor or grater, grate cheese. Transfer to small serving bowl.
6. Add chicken breasts to boiling stock, reduce heat, and poach at a gentle simmer 10 minutes.
7. Using slotted spoon, transfer poached chicken to plate. Reserve stock. Allow chicken to cool until it can be easily handled.

8. Meanwhile, heat 2 tablespoons oil in large heavy-gauge sauté pan over medium heat until hot. Break vermicelli into 3-inch lengths and cook in oil, stirring and tossing frequently, 2 minutes, or until browned. Using slotted spoon, transfer vermicelli to large serving dish; set aside.
9. Add remaining tablespoon oil to sauté pan. Add onion and garlic and cook over medium heat 2 to 3 minutes, or until onion is translucent.
10. Meanwhile, coarsely shred chicken.
11. Return vermicelli to pan and add reserved stock, cumin, and Cayenne. Cook over medium heat, covered, 4 minutes. Stir in shredded chicken, tomatoes, and bell pepper. Cook, covered, another 4 minutes, or until liquid is absorbed and vermicelli is tender.
12. Season sopa seca with salt to taste and transfer to large serving dish. Sprinkle with 1 tablespoon cheese and minced coriander. Serve remaining cheese on the side.

Cinco de Mayo Salad

Small head romaine lettuce
Small bunch fresh oregano, or ½ teaspoon dried
Medium-size zucchini
⅓ pound jícama
12 to 16 cherry tomatoes
½ cup good-quality olive oil
3 tablespoons white wine vinegar
1 tablespoon Dijon mustard
2 sprigs coriander for garnish (optional)

1. Wash romaine and dry in salad spinner or with paper towels. Remove and discard any bruised or discolored leaves. Place romaine in plastic bag and refrigerate until needed. Wash fresh oregano, if using, and pat dry. Mince enough oregano to measure 1½ teaspoons.
2. Wash and dry zucchini and jícama. Trim zucchini and cut crosswise into ¼-inch-thick slices; place in small nonaluminum bowl. Peel jícama and cut into 2-inch-long by ¼-inch-wide pieces; place in another small nonaluminum bowl.
3. Wash and dry cherry tomatoes; remove stems, if necessary. Halve tomatoes and set aside.
4. In medium-size nonaluminum bowl, combine oil, vinegar, mustard, and fresh or dried oregano, and whisk until well blended. Pour one third of dressing over zucchini, one third over jícama, and add cherry tomatoes to remaining dressing. Toss vegetables with dressing and let stand at least 10 minutes.
5. To serve, line serving platter with romaine leaves. Using slotted spoon, arrange vegetables in 3 rows on romaine leaves. Garnish with coriander sprigs, if desired.

Romaine lettuce

Three-Bean Chili
Garlic Toasts
Orange, Jícama, and Red Onion Salad

Colorful garnishes dress up a bowl of bean chili served with garlic toasts, salad, and a glass of ice-cold beer.

78

The unusual vegetarian chili comprises three varieties of beans. Red kidney beans are large and kidney shaped and have a meaty flavor. Black beans, also known as turtle beans, are small and flat with one white spot on their charcoal-colored skin. Pinto beans are medium-size pinkish-tan ovals speckled with brown spots (*pinto* means "dappled" in Spanish); they have a mealy texture and a meaty flavor. All three varieties are sold canned at supermarkets.

WHAT TO DRINK

Chili and beer are perfect partners, whether you choose a light domestic lager or a dark Mexican brew.

SHOPPING LIST AND STAPLES

Medium-size head romaine lettuce
⅓ pound jícama
Small red onion
Small bunch scallions
4 medium-size cloves garlic
Small bunch coriander
2 medium-size navel oranges
½ pint sour cream
4 tablespoons unsalted butter
3 ounces Cheddar or Monterey Jack cheese
2 cups chicken stock, preferably homemade (see page 10), or canned
16-ounce can pinto beans
16-ounce can black beans
8¾-ounce can kidney beans
14½-ounce can stewed tomatoes
3½-ounce can pitted black olives
8-ounce jar hot Mexican salsa
3 tablespoons vegetable oil
2 tablespoons white wine vinegar
Long loaf French bread (baguette)
½ teaspoon ground cumin
Salt and freshly ground pepper

UTENSILS

Food processor (optional)
Large nonaluminum saucepan
Baking sheet
Small nonaluminum bowl
Colander
Small strainer
Salad spinner (optional)
Measuring cups and spoons
Chef's knife
Bread knife with serrated blade (optional)
Paring knife
Vegetable peeler
Grater (if not using food processor)
Whisk
Ladle

START-TO-FINISH STEPS

Thirty minutes ahead: Set out butter to come to room temperature for toasts recipe.

1. Follow chili recipe steps 1 through 4.
2. Follow salad recipe steps 1 through 5.
3. Follow toasts recipe steps 1 through 4.
4. While toasts bake, follow chili recipe step 5.
5. Follow toasts recipe step 5 and chili recipe step 6.
6. Follow toasts recipe step 6 and salad recipe step 6.
7. Follow chili recipe step 7, toasts recipe step 7, and serve with salad.

RECIPES

Three-Bean Chili

1 cup kidney beans
1 cup pinto beans
1 cup black beans
3 ounces Cheddar or Monterey Jack cheese
2 scallions
Small bunch coriander
¼ cup pitted black olives
14½-ounce can stewed tomatoes
2 cups chicken stock
2 tablespoons hot Mexican salsa, approximately
½ teaspoon ground cumin
½ teaspoon salt
⅓ cup sour cream

1. Drain beans in colander and rinse under cold running water; set aside to drain.
2. Using food processor fitted with steel blade, or grater, grate cheese; set aside.
3. Wash scallions and coriander and dry with paper towels. Thinly slice scallions and set aside. Coarsely chop enough coriander to measure 2 tablespoons and set aside; reserve remaining coriander for another use.
4. Drain olives in small strainer and slice into rings.
5. Combine beans, tomatoes and their juice, stock, 2 tablespoons salsa, and cumin in large nonaluminum saucepan. Stir to combine and bring to a boil over medium-high heat.
6. Reduce heat and simmer chili 5 minutes. Season with salt and more salsa, if desired.
7. To serve, ladle chili into 4 bowls and garnish with cheese, scallions, coriander, olives, and sour cream.

Garlic Toasts

Long loaf French bread (baguette)
4 medium-size cloves garlic
4 tablespoons unsalted butter, at room temperature

1. Preheat oven to 400 degrees.
2. Cut bread into twelve ½-inch-thick slices.
3. Peel garlic cloves and halve lengthwise. Rub both sides of each slice of bread with garlic.

4. Spread both sides of bread with butter, place on baking sheet, and bake 4 to 5 minutes, or until tops are toasted.
5. Turn toasts and bake another 4 to 5 minutes.
6. Turn off oven and keep toasts warm until ready to serve.
7. To serve, turn toasts into napkin-lined basket.

Orange, Jícama, and Red Onion Salad

Medium-size head romaine lettuce
Small red onion
2 medium-size navel oranges
⅓ pound jícama
3 tablespoons vegetable oil
2 tablespoons white wine vinegar
Salt and freshly ground pepper

1. Wash romaine and dry in salad spinner or with paper towels. Remove and discard any bruised or discolored leaves. Place romaine in plastic bag and refrigerate until needed.
2. Halve and peel onion. Cut two ⅛-inch-thick slices from center; reserve remaining onion for another use. Separate slices into rings; set aside.
3. Halve 1 orange crosswise and squeeze enough juice from one half to measure 1 tablespoon. Peel other half, removing pith completely, and cut crosswise into 4 slices. Peel remaining orange, removing pith completely, and cut crosswise into 8 slices.
4. Peel jícama and cut into 2-inch-long by ⅛-inch-wide pieces.

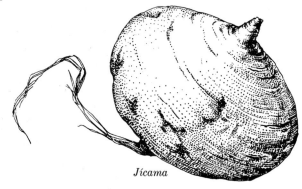
Jícama

5. Combine oil, vinegar, orange juice, and salt and pepper to taste in small nonaluminum bowl and whisk until blended; set aside until ready to serve.

6. To serve, line platter with romaine leaves. Top with jícama. Place orange slices and onion rings on top of jícama. Whisk dressing briefly to recombine and drizzle over salad.

ADDED TOUCH

The use of evaporated and sweetened condensed milk gives this Tex-Mex flan a denser texture than its Spanish counterpart.

Coffee Flan

1 cup sugar
5 eggs, at room temperature
14½-ounce can evaporated milk
14-ounce can sweetened condensed milk
1 cup half-and-half
3 tablespoons coffee liqueur, such as Kahlúa
1½ teaspoons vanilla extract

1. Preheat oven to 350 degrees.
2. In large heavy-gauge skillet, heat sugar over medium-high heat until it begins to melt. Lower heat to medium and continue to cook, stirring occasionally at first and then constantly, 10 to 14 minutes, or until sugar has caramelized to walnut-brown color.
3. Working quickly, pour caramel into 2-quart baking dish or distribute evenly among ten 4-ounce ramekins. Rotate dish or ramekins quickly so caramel coats bottom and about one quarter of way up sides.
4. In food processor fitted with steel blade, or in blender, combine eggs, evaporated milk, sweetened condensed milk, half-and-half, liqueur, and vanilla extract. Process until well blended.
5. Pour custard into baking dish or ramekins. Place dish or ramekins in large baking pan. (Ramekins should not touch one another or sides of baking pan.) Pour enough hot water into pan to reach halfway up sides of dish or ramekins.
6. Bake small flans 30 to 40 minutes, large flan 1 hour and 20 minutes, or until knife inserted in center comes out clean.
7. Remove dish or ramekins from hot water bath and allow to cool slightly. Refrigerate at least 3 hours before unmolding.
8. To unmold, run thin knife around edge of each flan and invert onto serving platter or plates.

Black Bean Soup
Flour Tortillas with Avocado Butter
Margarita Cream

Flour tortillas and avocado butter make fine accompaniments for black bean soup. Lime-flavored margarita cream is the dessert.

Flour tortillas, the flatbread of northern Mexico, are made from wheat flour, vegetable shortening or lard, salt, and water. Fresh or frozen flour tortillas can be found in the dairy or frozen food section of most supermarkets. Refrigerate fresh tortillas tightly wrapped in plastic and use them within four days.

WHAT TO DRINK

For an interesting blend of flavors, serve your guests a well-chilled spicy Gewürztraminer from California, Oregon, or Alsace.

SHOPPING LIST AND STAPLES

½ pound cooked ham
Large ripe avocado (about ½ pound), preferably Hass variety
Large onion
Small bunch radishes
Small bunch scallions
2 large cloves garlic
Small bunch fresh oregano, or 1 teaspoon dried
Small bunch fresh thyme, or ¼ teaspoon dried
Small bunch fresh coriander

3 large limes
½ pint heavy cream
½ pint sour cream
2 tablespoons unsalted butter
8 fresh or frozen flour tortillas
3 cups chicken stock, preferably homemade (see page 10), or canned
Three 16-ounce cans black beans
14½-ounce can whole peeled tomatoes
2 tablespoons vegetable oil
¼ cup sugar
¾ teaspoon ground cumin
⅛ teaspoon Cayenne pepper, approximately
Salt and freshly ground pepper
¼ cup dry sherry
1½ tablespoons tequila
1½ tablespoons Triple Sec, or other orange liqueur
1 tablespoon light rum

UTENSILS

Food processor or blender
Electric mixer
Medium-size heavy-gauge skillet or griddle
Large nonaluminum saucepan
Large bowl
Colander
Strainer
Measuring cups and spoons
Chef's knife
Paring knife
Wooden spoon
Rubber spatula
Zester or grater
Metal tongs
Ladle

START-TO-FINISH STEPS

One hour ahead: If using frozen tortillas, set out to thaw.

Thirty minutes ahead: Place bowl and beaters in freezer to chill for margarita cream recipe. Set out butter to come to room temperature for tortillas recipe.

1. Wash and dry limes. Cut 4 thin slices from center of 1 lime and grate enough zest from 2 remaining limes to measure 2 tablespoons for margarita cream recipe.

Squeeze enough lime juice to measure 1½ teaspoons for tortillas recipe and 3½ tablespoons for margarita cream recipe.
2. Follow soup recipe steps 1 through 8.
3. While soup simmers, follow tortillas recipe steps 1 through 5.
4. Follow margarita cream recipe steps 1 and 2.
5. Follow tortillas recipe step 6, soup recipe step 9, and serve.
6. Serve margarita cream for dessert.

RECIPES

Black Bean Soup

Three 16-ounce cans black beans
Small bunch fresh oregano, or 1 teaspoon dried
Small bunch fresh thyme, or ¼ teaspoon dried
Small bunch fresh coriander
4 radishes
1 scallion
14½-ounce can whole peeled tomatoes
Large onion
2 large cloves garlic
½ pound cooked ham
2 tablespoons vegetable oil
3 cups chicken stock
¼ cup dry sherry
¾ teaspoon ground cumin
Salt and freshly ground pepper
⅓ cup sour cream

1. Drain beans in colander, rinse under cold running water, and set aside to drain.
2. Wash and dry fresh herbs, if using. Mince oregano to measure 1 tablespoon, thyme to measure ½ teaspoon, and coriander to measure 2 tablespoons; set aside. Reserve remaining herbs for another use.
3. Wash radishes and scallion and dry with paper towels. Trim radishes and cut into thin slices. Trim scallion and cut on the diagonal into ¼-inch-thick slices.
4. Drain tomatoes in strainer and chop coarsely.
5. Halve and peel onion and chop coarsely. Crush, peel, and mince garlic.
6. Cut ham into ¾-inch cubes.
7. Heat oil in large nonaluminum saucepan over medium heat until hot. Add onion and cook, stirring, 3 to 5 minutes, or until translucent. Add garlic and cook 1 minute.

8. Stir in oregano, thyme, beans, tomatoes, ham, stock, sherry, and cumin. Increase heat to high and bring to a boil. Reduce heat and simmer, uncovered, 15 to 20 minutes.
9. Add salt and pepper to taste. To serve, ladle soup into 4 bowls, garnish with sour cream, coriander, radishes, and scallions.

Flour Tortillas with Avocado Butter

Large ripe avocado (about ½ pound), preferably Hass variety
2 tablespoons unsalted butter, at room temperature
1½ teaspoons lime juice, approximately
⅛ teaspoon Cayenne pepper, approximately
Salt
8 fresh flour tortillas, or 8 frozen flour tortillas, thawed

1. Preheat oven to 200 degrees.
2. Halve avocado lengthwise and discard pit. Scoop out pulp with small spoon.
3. In food processor or blender, combine avocado, butter, 1½ teaspoons lime juice, and ⅛ teaspoon Cayenne, and process until smooth. Season with salt to taste, and add more lime juice and Cayenne, if desired.
4. Using tongs, hold tortillas, one at a time, over gas flame, turning frequently, 20 seconds, or until soft and hot. Or heat tortillas in ungreased medium-size heavy-gauge skillet or on ungreased griddle over medium-high heat until soft and hot. (If, before heating, tortillas seem dry and a little hard, dip your hands in water and rub surface of tortillas to moisten them and make them more flexible.)
5. Wrap tortillas in slightly dampened kitchen towel and keep warm in oven until ready to serve.
6. Divide avocado butter among 4 small plates. Roll tortillas and place 1 on each plate. Keep remaining tortillas warm in napkin-lined basket.

Margarita Cream

1 cup heavy cream
¼ cup sugar
2 tablespoons grated lime zest
3½ tablespoons lime juice
1½ tablespoons tequila
1½ tablespoons Triple Sec, or other orange liqueur
1 tablespoon light rum
4 thin lime slices

1. In chilled large bowl, combine cream, sugar, 1 tablespoon lime zest, lime juice, tequila, liqueur, and rum. Beat with electric mixer at high speed until cream forms soft peaks.
2. Halve lime slices. Mound cream in margarita glasses or stemmed dessert glasses. Garnish with lime slices and remaining lime zest. Refrigerate until ready to serve.

ADDED TOUCH

Corn tortilla chips and a piquant *salsa cruda* (raw tomato sauce) make a lively hors d'oeuvre. The sauce is best when fresh tomatoes are at their flavor peak.

Toasted Corn Tortilla Chips with Salsa Cruda

4 to 6 corn tortillas
1 tablespoon vegetable oil, approximately
Salt
Salsa Cruda (see following recipe)

1. Preheat oven to 350 degrees.
2. Rub both sides of tortillas with oil and sprinkle lightly with salt. Cut each tortilla into 6 wedges.
3. Place wedges on well-oiled baking sheet and bake 15 to 20 minutes, or until crisp. Serve with salsa cruda on top or for dipping.

Salsa Cruda

Large ripe tomato
Large scallion
Small fresh jalapeño or serrano chili
Medium-size clove garlic
Small lime
Small bunch coriander
1 teaspoon olive or vegetable oil
Salt

1. Wash and dry tomato, scallion, and chili. Core and coarsely chop tomato. Trim and finely chop scallion. Wearing rubber gloves, seed, derib, and mince chili.
2. Crush, peel, and mince garlic.
3. Squeeze enough lime juice to measure 1 teaspoon.
4. Wash and dry coriander. Finely chop enough to measure 1 tablespoon.
5. In small serving bowl, combine tomato, scallion, chili, garlic, lime juice, and oil. Stir to blend well.
6. Stir in coriander, season with salt to taste, and serve.

Nancy Verde Barr

MENU 1 (Left)
Baked Scamorze and Olives
Mushroom Soup with Meatballs
Mixed Salad

MENU 2
Shrimp in Green Sauce
Grapefruit Salad
Quick Minestrone

MENU 3
Celery, Mushroom, and Parmesan Salad
Chicken with Olives
Oranges with Custard Sauce

Nancy Barr is especially interested in recipes from southern Italy, which was her paternal grandparents' home. As a cooking teacher, her ambition is to familiarize Americans with the diversity of southern Italian food.

Her three menus introduce a medley of regional Italian dishes, with an emphasis on those from the south. Menu 1 begins with a hearty melted cheese and olive appetizer served from the individual gratin dishes in which it is baked. The main-course mushroom soup contains small meatballs (*polpettine* in Italian) made from pork and veal. The salad is the classic *insalata mista* served throughout the country and varied by local cooks according to what is freshest in the markets.

The second menu features minestrone, the ubiquitous Italian vegetable soup that often requires lengthy cooking. Nancy Barr's Neapolitan version uses pasta instead of beans or rice and takes less than an hour to prepare. Here, shrimp in green sauce and a grapefruit salad are served with the soup. If you prefer to present this menu in true Italian fashion, the cook suggests serving the shrimp as a first course and the salad after the soup.

In Menu 3, a vibrant chicken stew with black and green olives, red bell peppers, and Italian plum tomatoes is the filling entrée. It needs only a light mushroom and celery salad to refresh the palate. The dessert, oranges with custard sauce (*arance con crema*), is a variation on a typical Sicilian offering.

A bowl of hot mushroom soup with meatballs is a filling and nourishing meal for a chilly evening. Precede it with a unique appetizer of melted cheese and briny olives, and accompany the soup with a salad that includes fennel, radicchio, and peppers.

85

Baked Scamorze and Olives
Mushroom Soup with Meatballs
Mixed Salad

The interesting appetizer for this menu calls for Scamorze, an Italian cheese of the type known as *pasta filata*, or "drawn curd." Scamorze is pear shaped and has a mild, slightly salty taste. If you prefer, bake the cheese slices on a large decorative platter instead of in individual dishes. The appetizer is eaten by spreading the melted cheese and olives on slices of toasted bread.

The mixed salad includes two popular Italian vegetables, *radicchio* and fennel. *Radicchio* is a ruby-red chicory with a slightly bitter but agreeable taste. It is generally available in the fall and winter; at other times of year, you can use red leaf lettuce or red cabbage instead. Fennel, also known as Florence fennel or anise, resembles a flattened bunch of celery with a bulbous base, long white stalks, and feathery green leaves. It has a distinctive yet faint taste of licorice.

WHAT TO DRINK

A light and simple red wine is a good first choice here. Candidates include a young Chianti or Barbera from Italy, a young Zinfandel or Gamay Beaujolais from California, or a red wine such as Chinon or Saumur-Champigny from France's Loire region.

SHOPPING LIST AND STAPLES

¼ pound ground pork tenderloin
¼ pound ground veal shoulder
1 pound fresh mushrooms
Small head romaine lettuce (about ¾ pound)
2 heads radicchio or red leaf lettuce (about 10 ounces total weight)
Large fennel bulb (about ¾ pound)
2 medium-size red bell peppers (about ½ pound total weight)
2 small tomatoes (about ½ pound total weight)
Medium-size carrot
Small onion
4 medium-size cloves garlic
Small bunch fresh oregano, or 1 tablespoon dried
Small bunch fresh basil, or 1 tablespoon dried
Small bunch fresh thyme, or 1 teaspoon dried
Small bunch fresh marjoram, or 2 teaspoons dried
1 egg
¾ pound Scamorze or mild Provolone cheese

2½ cups beef stock, or 1¼ cups each chicken and beef stock, preferably homemade (see page 10), or canned
7-ounce jar Gaeta or Kalamata olives
2-ounce tin flat anchovy fillets
16-ounce can Italian plum tomatoes
1¼ cups good-quality olive oil
2½ tablespoons red wine vinegar
Small loaf Italian bread
2 slices firm white bread
Salt
Freshly ground pepper

UTENSILS

Food processor (optional)
Large saucepan with cover
4 individual gratin dishes
Large salad bowl
Medium-size bowl
3 small bowls
Salad spinner (optional)
Colander
Large strainer
Small strainer
Measuring cups and spoons
Chef's knife
Paring knife
Wooden spoon
Grater (if not using food processor)
Pastry brush
Ladle

START-TO-FINISH STEPS

1. Wash fresh herbs, if using, and pat dry with paper towels. Mince enough oregano to measure 3 tablespoons for Scamorze recipe. Mince enough basil to measure 3 tablespoons, enough thyme to measure 1 tablespoon, and enough marjoram to measure 2 tablespoons for soup recipe.
2. Follow salad recipe step 1 and Scamorze recipe steps 1 through 4.
3. Follow soup recipe steps 1 through 7, Scamorze recipe steps 5 through 7, and salad recipe steps 2 and 3.
4. Follow Scamorze recipe step 8 and serve as first course.
5. Follow salad recipe steps 4 and 5, soup recipe step 8, and serve.

Baked Scamorze and Olives

20 Gaeta or Kalamata olives
4 flat anchovy fillets
Small loaf Italian bread
¾ pound Scamorze or mild Provolone cheese
¾ cup good-quality olive oil
3 tablespoons minced fresh oregano, or 1 tablespoon
    dried
Freshly ground pepper

1. Preheat oven to 450 degrees.
2. Drain olives in colander. Remove and discard pits. Drain anchovies in small strainer. Cut bread into eight ½-inch-thick slices; set aside.
3. Cut cheese lengthwise into four ½-inch-thick slices.
4. Divide 2 tablespoons olive oil among 4 individual gratin dishes. Place one slice of cheese in each dish and top each with 5 olives.
5. In small bowl, mash anchovies into a paste with fork. Stir in oregano and beat in ½ cup olive oil. Pour mixture over cheese and olives and sprinkle with pepper to taste.
6. Bake Scamorze 6 to 8 minutes, or until cheese is runny and slightly browned at edges.
7. Meanwhile, place bread in oven and toast, turning slices once, 5 to 7 minutes, or until lightly browned. Remove toasts and Scamorze from oven and brush one side of each toast with some of remaining 2 tablespoons olive oil.
8. Serve Scamorze with toasts.

Mushroom Soup with Meatballs

Small onion
3 medium-size cloves garlic
1 pound fresh mushrooms
16-ounce can Italian plum tomatoes
2 slices firm white bread
1 egg
3 tablespoons good-quality olive oil
Salt and freshly ground pepper
¼ pound ground pork tenderloin
¼ pound ground veal shoulder
2½ cups beef stock, or 1¼ cups each chicken and beef
    stock
3 tablespoons minced fresh basil, or 1 tablespoon dried
2 tablespoons minced fresh marjoram, or 2 teaspoons
    dried
1 tablespoon minced fresh thyme, or 1 teaspoon dried

1. Peel and coarsely chop onion; set aside. Crush, peel, and mince garlic; set aside. Wipe mushrooms clean with damp paper towels. Cut mushrooms into ¼-inch-thick slices; set aside. Drain tomatoes in large strainer and measure 2 cups; reserve juice and any remaining tomatoes for another use.
2. Using food processor or grater, grate enough bread to measure ¾ cup crumbs; set aside. Break egg into small

bowl and beat lightly with fork; set aside.
3. Heat oil in large saucepan over low heat. Add onion and garlic and cook 2 minutes, or until softened.
4. Add mushrooms, and salt and pepper to taste. Increase heat to high and cook, stirring occasionally, 6 to 8 minutes, or until mushroom juices have evaporated.
5. Meanwhile, combine bread crumbs, pork, and veal in medium-size bowl; add beaten egg and mix until well blended. Add ¼ teaspoon salt and ⅛ teaspoon pepper. Form mixture into about 20 walnut-size meatballs.
6. Add tomatoes to saucepan and cook over high heat, stirring occasionally, 5 minutes.
7. Add stock and bring to a boil. Add meatballs and herbs, reduce heat, and simmer, partially covered, 30 minutes.
8. Just before serving, season soup with salt and pepper to taste. Ladle soup into 4 bowls.

Mixed Salad

Medium-size clove garlic
Small head romaine lettuce (about ¾ pound)
2 heads radicchio or red leaf lettuce (about 10 ounces total
    weight)
Large fennel bulb (about ¾ pound)
2 medium-size red bell peppers (about ½ pound total
    weight)
2 small tomatoes (about ½ pound total weight)
Medium-size carrot
5 tablespoons good-quality olive oil
2½ tablespoons red wine vinegar
Salt and freshly ground pepper

1. Peel and halve garlic clove and rub inside of large salad bowl (preferably wood) with cut sides of clove. Discard garlic. Wash lettuce and radicchio and dry in salad spinner or with paper towels. Tear leaves into bite-size pieces. Place lettuce and radicchio in bowl.

Radicchio

2. Trim tops and bottom of fennel and cut bulb crosswise into ¼-inch-thick slices; place slices in bowl.
3. Wash and dry bell peppers, tomatoes, and carrot. Cut ½ inch from top of each pepper. Seed, derib, and cut peppers crosswise into ¼-inch-thick rings. Core tomatoes and cut each into 8 wedges. Trim and peel carrot. Using food processor or grater, grate carrot. Place vegetables in salad bowl and toss lightly to combine. Cover bowl with plastic wrap and refrigerate until ready to serve.
4. Just before serving, combine olive oil, vinegar, and salt and pepper to taste in small bowl and beat with fork until well blended.
5. Drizzle dressing over salad, toss to coat, and serve salad from bowl or on individual plates.

Shrimp in Green Sauce
Grapefruit Salad
Quick Minestrone

Quick minestrone soup, shrimp in green sauce, and a grapefruit, onion, and olive salad make an impressive lunch or supper.

The cook adds the unsmoked Italian bacon known as *pancetta* to the quick minestrone. *Pancetta* is a tightly rolled piece of pork cured in salt and spices. Look for it in Italian groceries and specialty food stores. Refrigerated tightly wrapped in plastic, it keeps for up to three weeks. If you cannot find *pancetta*, substitute any unsmoked ham. If yellow squash is unavailable, use two zucchini instead.

WHAT TO DRINK

A dry and crisp white wine would make the best accompaniment for these dishes. Try an Italian Verdicchio, a French Muscadet, or a California Sauvignon Blanc.

SHOPPING LIST AND STAPLES

¼ pound pancetta
1 pound fresh or frozen medium-size shrimp
Small bunch celery
2 medium-size carrots (about 6 ounces total weight)

Medium-size zucchini
Medium-size yellow squash
Small head Savoy cabbage
Small head chicory
Small red onion
Small yellow onion
Small clove garlic
Small bunch flat-leaf parsley
Small bunch fresh mint
Small bunch fresh oregano, or 2 teaspoons dried
Small bunch fresh thyme, or 1 teaspoon dried
2 small white or pink grapefruit
3 medium-size lemons
2 ounces Pecorino Romano cheese
2½ cups beef stock, or 1¼ cups each chicken and beef stock, preferably homemade (see page 10), or canned
2-ounce tin flat anchovy fillets, or 1 teaspoon anchovy paste
2-ounce jar imported capers
16-ounce can Italian plum tomatoes
7-ounce jar Gaeta olives

88

¾ cup good-quality olive oil
¼ pound small dried pasta, such as cavatelli
Salt
Freshly ground pepper

UTENSILS

Food processor or blender
4-quart stockpot with cover
Large saucepan with cover
Small saucepan
2 large nonaluminum bowls
Colander
Small strainer
Measuring cups and spoons
Chef's knife
Paring knife
2 wooden spoons
Rubber spatula
Grater (if not using food processor)
Ladle

START-TO-FINISH STEPS

1. Halve 2 lemons and squeeze enough juice to measure 5 tablespoons for shrimp recipe and 1 tablespoon for salad recipe. Peel onions. Halve red onion and thinly slice one half into rings for salad recipe. Mince enough of remaining half to measure 2 tablespoons for shrimp recipe. Dice yellow onion for minestrone recipe.
2. Follow minestrone recipe steps 1 through 7.
3. While soup simmers, follow shrimp recipe steps 1 and 2 and salad recipe steps 1 through 3.
4. Follow shrimp recipe step 3 and salad recipe step 4.
5. Follow shrimp recipe steps 4 through 8.
6. Follow salad recipe steps 5 and 6.
7. Follow minestrone recipe steps 8 and 9.
8. Follow salad recipe step 7, shrimp recipe step 9, minestrone recipe step 10, and serve.

RECIPES

Shrimp in Green Sauce

1 pound fresh or frozen medium-size shrimp
Medium-size carrot
Medium-size stalk celery, with leaves
3 tablespoons lemon juice
2 teaspoons salt
1 lemon for garnish

Green Sauce:
Small bunch flat-leaf parsley
2 tablespoons capers
Small clove garlic
3 flat anchovy fillets, or 1 teaspoon anchovy paste
2 tablespoons minced red onion
2 tablespoons lemon juice
6 tablespoons good-quality olive oil

Salt
Freshly ground pepper

1. If using fresh shrimp, pinch off legs several at a time, then bend back and snap off sharp, beaklike pieces of shell just above tail. Remove shell, except for tail, and discard. Using sharp paring knife, make shallow incision along back of each shrimp, exposing digestive vein. Extract vein and discard.

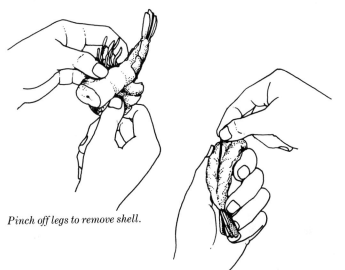

Pinch off legs to remove shell.

Extract digestive vein with your fingers.

2. Wash carrot and celery. Trim carrot. Place carrot, celery, lemon juice, salt, and 2 quarts water in 4-quart stockpot. Cover and bring to a boil over high heat.
3. Add fresh or frozen shrimp and return to a boil. Remove from heat and let stand 3 minutes.
4. Turn shrimp into colander and drain. Discard celery and carrot.
5. Quarter lemon for garnish; set aside.
6. For green sauce, wash and dry parsley and cut enough sprigs to measure ½ cup. Rinse capers in small strainer and drain. Crush and peel garlic.
7. In food processor fitted with steel blade, or in blender, combine parsley sprigs, capers, garlic, anchovies or anchovy paste, onion, and lemon juice. Process until well blended. With machine running, add olive oil in a slow steady stream and process until smooth. Season with salt and pepper to taste.
8. Turn shrimp into large nonaluminum bowl, add sauce, and toss until well coated. Set aside until ready to serve.
9. Just before serving, divide shrimp among 4 plates and garnish each plate with a lemon wedge.

Grapefruit Salad

Small head chicory
Small bunch mint
12 Gaeta olives
½ small red onion, cut into thin rings
2 small white or pink grapefruit

1 tablespoon lemon juice
3 tablespoons good-quality olive oil
Salt and freshly ground pepper

1. Wash and dry chicory. Separate leaves, place leaves in plastic bag, and refrigerate until needed. Wash mint and dry with paper towels. Remove enough mint leaves from stems to measure ¼ cup; set aside.
2. Drain olives in small strainer. Remove and discard pits.
3. Bring 3 cups water to a boil in small saucepan.
4. Add onion rings to boiling water and blanch 5 seconds. Turn into colander and refresh under cold running water. Pat onion rings dry with paper towels.
5. Working over large nonaluminum bowl to catch juice, peel grapefruit, removing all of white pith, and cut between membranes to separate segments. Drop segments into bowl as they are cut.
6. Add mint, onion rings, lemon juice, olive oil, and salt and pepper to taste to bowl with grapefruit and toss gently to combine. Cover and refrigerate salad until ready to serve.
7. Just before serving, line 4 plates with chicory. Top with grapefruit salad and garnish with olives.

Quick Minestrone

¼ pound pancetta
Medium-size carrot
Medium-size stalk celery
3 tablespoons good-quality olive oil
Small yellow onion, diced
Medium-size zucchini
Medium-size yellow squash
Small bunch fresh oregano, or 2 teaspoons dried
Small bunch fresh thyme, or 1 teaspoon dried
Salt
Freshly ground pepper
Small head Savoy cabbage
16-ounce can Italian plum tomatoes
2½ cups beef stock, or 1¼ cups each chicken and beef stock
¼ pound small dried pasta, such as cavatelli
2 ounces Pecorino Romano cheese

1. Mince pancetta; set aside. Wash, dry, trim, and finely dice carrot and celery; set aside.
2. Heat oil in large saucepan over medium-low heat. Add pancetta and cook 3 minutes.
3. Add carrot, celery, and onion, and cook over medium heat 7 minutes, or until softened but not browned.
4. Meanwhile, wash, dry, and trim zucchini and yellow squash. Cut crosswise into ¼-inch-thick slices; set aside. Wash and dry fresh oregano and thyme, if using. Finely chop enough oregano to measure 2 tablespoons and enough thyme to measure 1 tablespoon; set aside.
5. Add zucchini and yellow squash to pan, season with salt and pepper to taste, and cook 5 minutes.
6. Meanwhile, halve, core, and wash cabbage; dry with paper towels. Shred enough cabbage to measure 1 cup.

Reserve remaining cabbage for another use.
7. Add cabbage to pan and cook 2 minutes, or just until wilted. Add tomatoes and their juice, fresh or dried herbs, and salt and pepper to taste, and stir to break up tomatoes. Add stock, bring to a boil, reduce heat, and simmer soup 25 minutes.
8. Add pasta and cook soup, partially covered, another 12 to 15 minutes, or until pasta is tender.
9. Meanwhile, using food processor fitted with steel blade, or grater, grate cheese.
10. Ladle soup into 4 bowls and serve with grated cheese on the side.

ADDED TOUCH

This rich cheese pudding is equally good served hot from the baking dish or cooled. In either case, the pudding will sink slightly in the center.

Budino di Ricotta

½ cup candied fruit
¼ cup Maraschino liqueur or rum
Medium-size lemon
4 eggs
1 pound ricotta cheese
½ cup plus 2 tablespoons granulated sugar
2 tablespoons all-purpose flour
⅛ teaspoon ground nutmeg
1 tablespoon unsalted butter
2 teaspoons confectioners' sugar

1. Preheat oven to 350 degrees.
2. Combine candied fruit and Maraschino liqueur or rum in small bowl and macerate 1 hour.
3. Wash and dry lemon. Grate enough rind to measure 1 tablespoon.
4. Separate 3 eggs, placing whites in large copper or stainless-steel bowl and yolks in second large bowl.
5. Add ricotta to yolks and beat well. Add remaining whole egg and beat well.
6. Beat in ½ cup granulated sugar, flour, lemon rind, and nutmeg. Stir in candied fruit and liqueur or rum.
7. Beat egg whites with electric mixer at high speed, or with whisk, until stiff peaks form. With rubber spatula, stir one quarter of whites into ricotta mixture, then gently fold in remaining whites.
8. Butter 2-quart mold and dust with remaining 2 tablespoons granulated sugar. Pour in ricotta mixture and bake 45 minutes, or until puffed and golden.
9. Serve hot from mold, or allow to cool and unmold onto serving platter. Sift confectioners' sugar over top.

LEFTOVER SUGGESTION

Store any leftover green sauce in a tightly closed container in the refrigerator. It makes a delicious sauce for poached fish or hard-boiled eggs. Be sure to bring it to room temperature before serving.

Celery, Mushroom, and Parmesan Salad
Chicken with Olives
Oranges with Custard Sauce

A Parmesan-topped salad goes well with zesty chicken and olive stew. Serve oranges in custard sauce for dessert.

This southern Italian meal features a dessert that would typically be made with blood oranges. Here, the more readily available navel oranges are used and flavored with Maraschino liqueur. This Italian liqueur, made from the sour Marasca cherry, is clear and has an intense cherry flavor. You can substitute rum, brandy, or vanilla extract if you prefer.

WHAT TO DRINK

This menu calls for a full-bodied white wine with plenty of fruit. An Italian or California Chardonnay, or French white Burgundy (a Mâcon wine or a simple Chablis) would be good.

SHOPPING LIST AND STAPLES

8 chicken legs (about 3 pounds total weight)
Large bunch celery (about 1½ pounds total weight)
6 ounces large fresh mushrooms
2 medium-size red bell peppers (about ½ pound total weight)
Medium-size yellow onion
3 medium-size cloves garlic
Small bunch fresh oregano, or 1 teaspoon dried
Small bunch fresh thyme, or ½ teaspoon dried
3 large navel oranges
Medium-size lemon
3 eggs
¾ cup milk
3 ounces Parmesan cheese, preferably imported
⅓ cup chicken stock, preferably homemade (see page 10), or canned
6-ounce can pitted black olives
5¾-ounce can pitted green olives
2-ounce tin flat anchovy fillets (optional)
16-ounce can Italian plum tomatoes
½ cup plus 1 tablespoon good-quality olive oil
2 tablespoons red wine vinegar
1 tablespoon all-purpose flour
1 cup sugar, approximately
¼ teaspoon red pepper flakes
Salt
Freshly ground pepper
½ cup dry red wine
6 tablespoons Maraschino liqueur, rum, or brandy

UTENSILS

Large skillet with cover
2 small saucepans, 1 heavy-gauge with cover
Double boiler
Large bowl
Heatproof serving bowl
Strainer
Measuring cups and spoons
Chef's knife
Paring knife
2 wooden spoons
Citrus juicer (optional)
Whisk
Metal tongs
Vegetable peeler
Candy thermometer

START-TO-FINISH STEPS

1. Halve lemon and squeeze enough juice from one half to measure 2 tablespoons for salad recipe; reserve remaining half for oranges recipe.
2. Follow chicken recipe steps 1 through 5.
3. While chicken is browning, follow oranges recipe steps 1 and 2 and salad recipe steps 1 through 3.
4. Follow chicken recipe steps 6 through 8.
5. While chicken simmers, follow oranges recipe steps 3 through 8.
6. Follow chicken recipe step 9 and salad recipe steps 4 and 5.
7. Follow chicken recipe step 10 and serve with salad.
8. Follow oranges recipe step 9 and serve for dessert.

RECIPES

Celery, Mushroom, and Parmesan Salad

Large bunch celery (about 1½ pounds total weight)
6 ounces large fresh mushrooms
3 ounces Parmesan cheese, preferably imported
2 tablespoons lemon juice
5 tablespoons good-quality olive oil
Salt and freshly ground pepper

1. Wash celery and dry with paper towels. Trim ends, and peel stalks to remove strings. Cut enough celery on the diagonal into ⅛-inch-thick slices to measure about 4 cups.
2. Wipe mushrooms clean with damp paper towels. Cut into ⅛-inch-thick slices.
3. Using chef's knife, cut Parmesan into slivers.
4. Scatter celery on serving platter and top with mushrooms. Mound Parmesan in center.
5. Sprinkle lemon juice, olive oil, and salt and pepper to taste over salad. Toss salad before serving.

Chicken with Olives

Medium-size yellow onion
3 medium-size cloves garlic
2 medium-size red bell peppers (about ½ pound total weight)
Small bunch fresh oregano, or 1 teaspoon dried
Small bunch fresh thyme, or ½ teaspoon dried
4 flat anchovy fillets (optional)
½ cup pitted black olives
½ cup pitted green olives
¼ cup good-quality olive oil
8 chicken legs (about 3 pounds total weight)
½ teaspoon salt

1 tablespoon all-purpose flour
½ cup dry red wine
⅓ cup chicken stock
2 tablespoons red wine vinegar
16-ounce can Italian plum tomatoes
⅛ to ¼ teaspoon red pepper flakes

1. Peel onion and cut crosswise into ¼-inch-thick rings. Crush and peel garlic.
2. Wash bell peppers and dry with paper towels. Core, halve, and seed peppers. Quarter pepper halves.
3. Wash fresh herbs, if using, and pat dry with paper towels. Mince enough oregano to measure 1 tablespoon and enough thyme to measure 1½ teaspoons.
4. If using anchovies, rinse under cold running water, drain in strainer, and chop finely. Drain black and green olives in strainer.
5. Heat olive oil in large skillet over medium-high heat until hot. Add chicken legs and cook, turning once, 10 to 15 minutes, or until browned on all sides.
6. Using tongs, transfer chicken to large plate and sprinkle with salt.
7. Add onion, garlic, and bell peppers to skillet, reduce heat to medium, cover, and cook 5 minutes.
8. Sprinkle vegetables with flour and cook, stirring, another 3 minutes. Add wine, stock, vinegar, tomatoes and 2 or 3 tablespoons of their juice, oregano, thyme, and red pepper flakes. Increase heat to high and bring mixture to a boil. Add chicken, reduce heat, and simmer, covered, 20 minutes.
9. Add olives, and anchovies if using, and cook, uncovered, another 10 to 15 minutes, or until juices run clear when chicken is pierced with knife.
10. Transfer chicken, vegetables, and sauce to large platter and serve.

Oranges with Custard Sauce

3 large navel oranges
3 eggs
⅔ cup plus ¼ cup sugar
½ lemon
6 tablespoons Maraschino liqueur, rum, or brandy
¾ cup milk

1. Peel oranges, removing all of white pith, and cut crosswise into ¼-inch-thick slices. Place in heatproof serving bowl; set aside.
2. Separate eggs, placing yolks in large bowl and reserving whites for another use.
3. Combine ⅓ cup water, ⅔ cup sugar, and 2 drops lemon juice in small heavy-gauge saucepan. Cover and cook over high heat 3 minutes, or until sugar is melted and liquid is not cloudy. Uncover and cook another 3 minutes, or until syrup registers 230 degrees on candy thermometer. Immediately add 4 tablespoons Maraschino liqueur, rum, or brandy and swirl pan to combine. Pour syrup over oranges, turning to coat, and refrigerate until ready to serve.

4. Meanwhile, heat milk in another small saucepan over medium-low heat until warm.
5. Bring 1 to 2 inches of water to a simmer in bottom of double boiler.
6. Add remaining ¼ cup sugar to egg yolks in large bowl and beat with wooden spoon just until blended. Continuing to beat with wooden spoon, slowly drizzle warm milk into egg mixture.
7. Place mixture in top of double boiler and set over, but not in, simmering water. Cook over low heat, stirring constantly with wooden spoon, 3 to 4 minutes, or until foam subsides and custard coats back of spoon.
8. Remove top of double boiler and whisk custard sauce until slightly cooled. Strain custard sauce into pitcher and add remaining 2 tablespoons Maraschino liqueur, rum, or brandy; set aside.
9. To serve, pour some of custard sauce over oranges and serve remaining sauce in pitcher.

ADDED TOUCH

Finger-length strips of fried eggplant baked with typical Italian seasonings make a satisfying side dish.

Fried and Baked Eggplant

2 small eggplants (about 1½ pounds total weight)
Salt
3 medium-size cloves garlic
Small bunch fresh oregano, or 1 tablespoon dried
2 cups good-quality olive oil, approximately
2 tablespoons red wine vinegar

1. Preheat oven to 350 degrees.
2. Wash eggplants and dry with paper towels. Trim tops and bottoms and cut eggplants lengthwise into ½-inch-thick slices. Halve each slice crosswise, then cut lengthwise into ¾-inch-wide strips.
3. Place eggplant in colander, sprinkle with salt, and allow to drain 1 hour.
4. Meanwhile, peel and mince garlic. Wash fresh oregano, if using, and pat dry with paper towels. Mince enough oregano to measure 3 tablespoons. Line platter with double thickness of paper towels.
5. After eggplant has drained, rinse, and dry with paper towels. Heat olive oil in deep straight-sided skillet over medium-high heat until very hot. Add a few eggplant strips and cook, turning occasionally, 2 to 3 minutes, or until golden. Using slotted spatula, transfer eggplant to paper-towel-lined platter. Cook remaining eggplant strips in same manner.
6. Spread one third of eggplant strips in 8-inch square baking dish and sprinkle with one third of garlic, one third of vinegar, one third of oregano, and salt to taste. Layer remaining ingredients in same manner.
7. Bake eggplant 15 minutes. Using slotted spatula, transfer eggplant to serving platter and serve hot or at room temperature.

Paul Heroux

H aving worked as a professional cook for the past ten years, and now a ceramist, Paul Heroux finds that cooking is just as much an art as pottery-making: "I put as much energy into carefully combining the flavors and colors of ingredients as I put into my sculpturing," he says. He concentrates on creating meals built on regional themes, then judiciously introduces elements from other cuisines. Because he has lived in Massachusetts and Maine, he often turns to New England favorites for his inspiration.

The Menu 1 chowder, dotted with bright vegetables, is a straightforward coastal dish containing lobster meat, clams, and corn. Here it is enriched by the addition of vermouth. The accompanying homemade biscuits, a traditional partner with chowder, are flavored with scallions.

Paul Heroux describes Menu 3 as a meal New Englanders might prepare from late summer to early winter. It includes broiled oysters on the half shell topped with two savory sauces—a lemony tomato relish and a garlic-herb butter—and served with a rich chicken and vegetable stew. The stew can be presented in hollowed-out squash, as suggested, or in a simple tureen.

As a change of pace, Menu 2 combines European and Oriental features. The soup is a beef broth fortified with dumplings that are flavored, in the Italian manner, with thyme and basil. The salad combines Japanese *soba* noodles with sliced almonds and bell peppers. You can serve the soup and salad together, or as two courses.

Capture the flavors of New England with lobster, clam, and corn chowder and flaky scallion biscuits. Keep extra biscuits warm in the oven.

Lobster Chowder with Clams and Corn
Scallion Biscuits

The chowder calls for North American lobsters, which are prized for their rich meat. Buy only live lobsters that are very active in the tank, and choose two of approximately the same size, so they will cook uniformly. Do not buy precooked lobsters, or any variety of imported lobster, because they lack the sweetness necessary for this dish.

If shucked clams are not available, shuck your own, or use shucked oysters or mussels, or a combination of the two, instead.

WHAT TO DRINK

Either a California Sauvignon Blanc or a French Muscadet would go well with the chowder.

SHOPPING LIST AND STAPLES

Two 1¼-pound North American lobsters
24 shucked fresh small clams, such as littlenecks, or 10-ounce can whole small clams
2 medium-size leeks (about 1½ pounds total weight)
Medium-size fennel bulb with at least 4 stalks (about ½ pound), if available
Small bunch celery plus ½ teaspoon fennel seeds, if not using fresh fennel
3 medium-size parsnips (½ to ¾ pound total weight)
Small ripe tomato
Small bunch scallions
1 envelope dry yeast
2 cups milk
1 pint heavy cream
1 stick plus 3 tablespoons unsalted butter, approximately
10-ounce package frozen corn kernels
3 cups chicken stock, preferably homemade (see page 10), or canned
2¾ cups all-purpose flour, approximately
2½ teaspoons double-acting baking powder
1 teaspoon baking soda
½ teaspoon dried thyme
½ teaspoon sweet paprika
Salt
Freshly ground black pepper
Coarsely ground black pepper (optional)
½ cup dry vermouth

UTENSILS

Large heavy-gauge nonaluminum stockpot with tight-fitting cover
Large heavy-gauge nonaluminum saucepan
17 x 11-inch baking sheet
2 large bowls
2 small bowls
Colander
Large fine strainer
Flour sifter or sieve
Measuring cups and spoons
Chef's knife
Paring knife
2 wooden spoons
Metal spatula
Whisk
Metal tongs
Rolling pin
Vegetable peeler
Nutcracker
Pastry blender (optional)

START-TO-FINISH STEPS

Thirty minutes ahead: Set out 3 tablespoons butter to come to room temperature for biscuits recipe. Remove enough frozen corn to measure 1 cup for chowder recipe; return remaining corn to freezer.

1. Follow chowder recipe steps 1 through 5.
2. While lobsters cool, follow biscuits recipe steps 1 through 8.
3. While biscuits are baking, follow chowder recipe steps 6 and 7.
4. Follow biscuits recipe step 9 and chowder recipe steps 8 through 10.
5. Follow biscuits recipe step 10.
6. Follow chowder recipe steps 11 and 12 and serve with biscuits.

RECIPES

Lobster Chowder with Clams and Corn

3 cups chicken stock
½ cup dry vermouth
2 medium-size leeks (about 1½ pounds total weight)

Medium-size fennel bulb with at least 4 stalks, or
    4 medium-size celery stalks plus ½ teaspoon
    fennel seeds
½ teaspoon dried thyme
½ teaspoon sweet paprika
Two 1¼-pound North American lobsters
3 medium-size parsnips (½ to ¾ pound total
    weight)
Small ripe tomato
5 tablespoons unsalted butter
¼ cup all-purpose flour
1 cup milk
2 cups heavy cream
24 shucked fresh small clams, such as littlenecks,
    or 1 cup canned whole small clams
1 cup frozen corn, thawed
Salt and freshly ground black pepper
Coarsely ground black pepper (optional)

1. In large heavy-gauge nonaluminum stockpot, bring chicken stock, vermouth, and 1 cup water to a boil over high heat.
2. Meanwhile, trim dark green leaves from leeks. Wash and coarsely chop leaves; reserve leeks. Wash fennel and remove 4 stalks; reserve bulb for another use. Coarsely chop 2 stalks; set aside remaining 2 stalks. Add chopped leek leaves, chopped fennel stalks, thyme, and paprika to stockpot.
3. When water boils, add lobsters. Cover pot, reduce heat to medium, and simmer 15 minutes; do *not* boil lobsters.
4. Meanwhile, trim root end of leeks and halve leeks lengthwise. Wash thoroughly under cold running water to remove sand and grit, and dry with paper towels. Split each leek in half lengthwise and cut crosswise into ¼-inch-wide pieces; set aside. Cut 2 reserved fennel stalks into ¼-inch-long pieces; set aside. Wash and peel parsnips and cut into ½-inch dice; set aside. Wash, core, seed, and coarsely chop tomato; set aside.
5. When lobsters have cooked 15 minutes, transfer with tongs to colander to drain and cool. Keep stock at a simmer.
6. When lobsters are cool enough to handle, remove meat from tail, legs, and claws, using nutcracker to crack claws. Return all shells to simmering stock for additional flavor. Using chef's knife, cut lobster meat into ½-inch chunks; set aside.
7. While stock continues to simmer, in large heavy-gauge nonaluminum saucepan melt 4 tablespoons butter over low heat. Add reserved leeks and fennel, and diced parsnips, and cook, stirring occasionally, about 5 minutes, or until softened. Remove pan from heat.
8. Turn stock into large fine strainer set over large bowl; discard solids. Measure stock and add enough hot water, if necessary, to make 5 cups.
9. Place saucepan with cooked vegetables over high heat. Add remaining 1 tablespoon butter, and flour, and cook, stirring constantly, 1 to 2 minutes, or until just blended. Add hot stock and whisk constantly, still over high heat,

until mixture comes to a boil. Stir in milk and cream, reduce heat to medium, and cook 2 to 3 minutes, or until heated through. Do not allow soup to boil.
10. Meanwhile, drain clams in strainer, if necessary.
11. Add lobster meat, tomatoes, clams, and corn to chowder and season with salt and pepper to taste. Cook, stirring occasionally, 3 minutes.
12. To serve, divide chowder among 4 bowls and sprinkle with coarsely ground black pepper, if desired.

Scallion Biscuits

1½ teaspoons dry yeast
2 medium-size scallions
3 tablespoons unsalted butter, at room temperature
2½ cups all-purpose flour, approximately
2½ teaspoons double-acting baking powder
1 teaspoon baking soda
½ teaspoon salt
3 tablespoons unsalted butter, well chilled
1 cup milk

1. Preheat oven to 450 degrees. Lightly butter 17 x 11-inch baking sheet.
2. In small bowl, stir yeast into 3 tablespoons warm (not hot) water. Set aside.
3. Wash scallions and dry with paper towels. Trim and finely chop enough to measure about ½ cup. Combine scallions with 3 tablespoons softened butter in small bowl; set aside.
4. In large bowl, sift together 2½ cups flour, baking powder, baking soda, and salt. Cut 3 tablespoons chilled butter into small pieces. Using pastry blender or two knives, cut butter into dry ingredients until mixture resembles coarse cornmeal.
5. Add milk and stir with fork until blended. Stir in yeast mixture and continue to mix lightly, tossing, until soft dough forms. Generously flour work surface and scrape dough onto it. Knead for a few seconds only, dusting dough with additional flour, if necessary, to prevent sticking; do not overhandle dough.
6. Working quickly, roll out dough and pat into 15 by 6-inch rectangle. Spread scallion butter evenly over dough and fold dough into thirds, as you would fold a letter. Turn dough so one long side is toward you, and roll out again into 15 by 6-inch rectangle. Fold dough into thirds again and turn so one long side is toward you. Roll out dough again and pat into 12 by 6-inch rectangle, ¾ to 1 inch thick. Using a sharp knife, trim about ¼ inch of dough from all edges.
7. Cut dough in half lengthwise. Cut each half into 4 equal squares. Using floured spatula, transfer biscuits to prepared baking sheet.
8. Bake biscuits 15 minutes, or until golden brown.
9. Turn off oven and leave biscuits in oven another 5 minutes to continue baking.
10. After 5 minutes, wrap biscuits in foil, return to oven, and keep warm on bottom rack until ready to serve.

Three-Meat Dumplings in Beef Broth with Tomatoes
Soba Noodle Salad

Clear soup with dumplings made from pork, chicken, and crab and soba *noodle salad are a sumptuous meal any time of year.*

Japanese *soba*, or buckwheat noodles, are the main ingredient in the salad. Made from buckwheat flour and gray-brown in color, these thin dried noodles may be round or flat. Look for them in health food stores and at Japanese groceries. Sautéing the almonds and bell peppers releases their flavors, thereby eliminating the need to marinate the salad for hours.

WHAT TO DRINK

A light red wine would add the perfect touch to this meal. A French Beaujolais or California Gamay Beaujolais is ideal.

SHOPPING LIST AND STAPLES

¼ pound ground pork
¼ pound boneless, skinless chicken breast
½ pound fresh or frozen lump crabmeat
Medium-size red bell pepper

Medium-size green bell pepper
Small bunch scallions
Small red onion
4 medium-size cloves garlic
1 egg
4 cups beef stock, preferably homemade (see page 10), or canned
8-ounce can peeled whole tomatoes
⅓ cup good-quality olive oil
3 tablespoons rice vinegar
1 tablespoon raspberry vinegar
1 tablespoon soy sauce
½ pound Japanese soba noodles or whole-wheat noodles
2-ounce jar pine nuts
3½-ounce can sliced almonds
1½ tablespoons cornstarch
1 bay leaf
½ teaspoon dried thyme
½ teaspoon dried basil
Salt
Freshly ground black pepper

¼ teaspoon freshly ground white pepper
½ cup light red wine, such as Beaujolais

UTENSILS

Food processor (optional)
Large stockpot or saucepan
Wok or large heavy-gauge skillet
Large nonaluminum saucepan with cover
Large bowl (if not using food processor)
Colander
Measuring cups and spoons
Chef's knife
Paring knife
2 wooden spoons
Ladle

START-TO-FINISH STEPS

1. Follow salad recipe steps 1 through 6.
2. Follow soup recipe steps 1 through 7.
3. Follow salad recipe step 7, soup recipe steps 8 and 9, and serve.

RECIPES

Three-Meat Dumplings in Beef Broth with Tomatoes

¼ pound boneless, skinless chicken breast
2 medium-size cloves garlic
3 scallions
1 egg
1½ tablespoons cornstarch
½ teaspoon dried thyme
½ teaspoon dried basil
¼ teaspoon freshly ground white pepper
½ pound fresh or frozen lump crabmeat
¼ pound ground pork
¼ cup pine nuts
½ cup light red wine, such as Beaujolais
4 cups beef stock
1 tablespoon raspberry vinegar
1 bay leaf
8-ounce can peeled whole tomatoes

1. Wash chicken breast and dry with paper towel. Cut chicken into 1-inch cubes; you should have about ¾ cup. Peel and halve garlic. Wash and trim scallions; cut off dark green tops and set aside for garnish. Cut white parts of scallions into 1-inch pieces. Separate egg, placing white in container of food processor or in large bowl, and reserving yolk for another use.
2. Add chicken, garlic, white parts of scallions, cornstarch, thyme, basil, and white pepper to food processor, if using, and pulse about 10 seconds, or until coarsely chopped. Or, mince chicken, garlic, and scallions with chef's knife; add to bowl with egg. Add cornstarch, thyme,

basil, and white pepper, and stir to combine.
3. Pick over crabmeat and remove any bits of shell or cartilage. Add crabmeat and pork to chicken mixture in processor and process 2 to 5 seconds, or just until combined. Or, add crabmeat and pork to bowl and stir to combine. Stir in pine nuts.
4. In large nonaluminum saucepan, combine wine, stock, vinegar, bay leaf, and juice from canned tomatoes, and bring to a simmer over medium heat.
5. Meanwhile, shape dumpling mixture into about forty 1½-inch balls.
6. Using teaspoon, drop dumplings into simmering liquid. Reduce heat to low and poach dumplings 15 minutes, or until cooked through.
7. Meanwhile, coarsely chop tomatoes. Thinly slice reserved scallion greens.
8. Stir tomatoes into soup and simmer 2 to 3 minutes, or until heated through. Remove and discard bay leaf.
9. Ladle soup and dumplings into 4 shallow soup bowls and garnish with sliced scallion greens.

Soba Noodle Salad

2 medium-size cloves garlic
Small red onion
Medium-size green bell pepper
Medium-size red bell pepper
½ pound Japanese soba noodles or whole-wheat noodles
⅓ cup good-quality olive oil
½ cup sliced almonds
1 tablespoon soy sauce
3 tablespoons rice vinegar
½ teaspoon salt
Freshly ground black pepper

1. In large stockpot or saucepan, bring 3 quarts water to a boil.
2. Meanwhile, crush and peel garlic; set aside. Peel onion and finely chop enough to measure 2 tablespoons. Wash and dry bell peppers. Halve peppers lengthwise and remove cores and seeds. Cut peppers lengthwise into thin slices; set aside.
3. Add noodles to boiling water and stir gently until water returns to a boil. Cook 5 minutes, or according to package directions, until *al dente*.
4. Meanwhile, in wok or large heavy-gauge skillet, heat oil over high heat. Add garlic and cook about 30 seconds, or until garlic is browned. Discard garlic and add bell peppers and almonds. Stir fry 1 to 2 minutes, or until almonds begin to brown. Add onion and stir fry, tossing, 1 minute. Remove wok or pan from heat and add soy sauce, vinegar, salt, and pepper to taste.
5. Turn noodles into colander, rinse under cold running water, and drain.
6. Add drained noodles to wok and toss to blend with sauce and vegetables; set aside until ready to serve.
7. To serve, divide salad among 4 plates or bowls.

Broiled Oysters with Two Sauces
Chicken and Vegetable Stew in Squash Bowls

Elegant oysters on the half shell are delicious with the chicken and vegetable stew presented in squash-shell bowls.

Often eaten raw, oysters can also be baked, roasted, fried, grilled—or broiled, as in this recipe. To shuck oysters yourself, first scrub the shells well under cold running water with a stiff-bristled brush. Then, wearing rubber gloves if desired, grasp the oyster in one hand with the hinged part of the shell in your palm. With the other hand, force the tip of an oyster knife between the shells near the hinge or into any seemingly penetrable place, being careful not to plunge the knife into the oyster meat. Once the knife is inserted, carefully slide it around the rim until you cut the muscle holding the shells together, then twist the knife to open the shells. Slide the knife along the lower shell to free the meat, discard the upper shell, and remove any bits of loose shell.

Serving the stew in hollowed-out buttercup squash gives this meal flair. For an interesting variation, make a tureen from a 5- or 6-pound pumpkin. Cut off the top third of the pumpkin and reserve it as a lid. Proceed as you would for the squash. When the meal is over, drain the pumpkin of any remaining soup. Peel and cube the flesh, which will have absorbed the flavors of the stock and wine, and steam until very tender. Purée the steamed pumpkin in a food processor or blender with some butter, ground cumin, salt, and a dash of Cayenne pepper. Serve the purée as a vegetable side dish at another meal.

WHAT TO DRINK

A dry, fruity white wine such as an Alsatian Riesling or a Pinot Blanc or Vouvray from the Loire would best complement this menu. A dry California Chenin Blanc is another possibility.

SHOPPING LIST AND STAPLES

2 whole boneless, skinless chicken
   breasts (about 1¼ pounds total weight)
16 oysters, shucked, with bottom shells
4 buttercup, butternut, acorn, or Hubbard squash
   (5 to 6 pounds total weight)
1 each small red and green bell pepper
Small ripe tomato
2 small cloves garlic
Small bunch parsley
Small lemon
6 tablespoons unsalted butter
10-ounce package frozen pearl onions
1¾ cups chicken stock, preferably homemade
   (see page 10), or canned
1 tablespoon good-quality olive oil
4 tablespoons corn oil
½ teaspoon tarragon vinegar
½ teaspoon Worcestershire sauce
¼ cup all-purpose flour
¼ cup whole yellow mustard seeds
½ teaspoon curry powder
½ teaspoon dried chervil

1 bay leaf
Salt
Kosher salt (optional)
Freshly ground black pepper
⅓ cup dry white wine

UTENSILS

Large heavy-gauge saucepan or Dutch oven, with cover
Roasting pan
17 x 11-inch baking sheet
9-inch pie pan
2 small bowls, 1 nonaluminum
Measuring cups and spoons
Chef's knife
Paring knife
2 wooden spoons
Slotted spoon
Metal spatula
Grater or zester
Whisk
Metal tongs
Ladle
Pastry brush

START-TO-FINISH STEPS

Thirty minutes ahead: Set out 5 tablespoons butter to come to room temperature for oysters recipe. Separate enough frozen onions to measure ½ cup for stew recipe and return remaining onions to freezer.

1. Follow stew recipe steps 1 through 5.
2. Follow oysters recipe steps 1 through 3.
3. Follow stew recipe steps 6 and 7 and oysters recipe steps 4 and 5.
4. Follow stew recipe steps 8 and 9.
5. Follow oysters recipe step 6 and stew recipe step 10.
6. Follow oysters recipe step 7, stew recipe 11, and serve.

RECIPES

Broiled Oysters with Two Sauces

Small ripe tomato
Small lemon
Small bunch parsley
2 small cloves garlic
¼ teaspoon freshly ground black pepper
½ teaspoon Worcestershire sauce
1 tablespoon good-quality olive oil
5 tablespoons unsalted butter, at room temperature
½ teaspoon dried chervil
½ teaspoon tarragon vinegar
16 oysters, shucked, with bottom shells
Kosher salt (optional)

1. Wash and dry tomato. Core and halve tomato and squeeze out seeds. Finely chop enough tomato to measure

½ cup. Wash and dry lemon. Using grater or zester, grate enough lemon zest to measure 1 teaspoon. Squeeze enough lemon juice to measure 2 teaspoons. Wash, dry, and finely chop enough parsley to measure 2 tablespoons. Peel garlic and chop enough to measure 1 teaspoon.

2. In small nonaluminum bowl, combine chopped tomato, lemon zest, lemon juice, pepper, Worcestershire sauce, and oil. Stir to mix well. Set aside.

3. In another small bowl, cream together butter, chopped parsley, garlic, chervil, and vinegar. Set aside.

4. Place oysters in shells on 17 x 11-inch baking sheet. (If you like, first spread a ½-inch layer of kosher salt on baking sheet. The salt will stabilize the shells and keep them from tipping.)

5. Dividing sauces equally, top one half of each oyster with tomato sauce, then spoon herbed butter onto other half.

6. Turn on broiler. Broil oysters 4 inches from heating element about 3 minutes, or until butter begins to brown and oysters are heated through.

7. Using tongs, carefully transfer 4 oysters to each of 4 small plates and serve.

Chicken and Vegetable Stew in Squash Bowls

4 buttercup, butternut, acorn, or Hubbard squash
(5 to 6 pounds total weight)
4 tablespoons corn oil
Small green bell pepper
Small red bell pepper
2 whole boneless, skinless chicken breasts (about
1¼ pounds total weight)
¼ cup whole yellow mustard seeds
¼ cup all-purpose flour
½ teaspoon curry powder
Pinch of salt
Freshly ground black pepper
½ cup frozen pearl onions, thawed
1 tablespoon unsalted butter
⅓ cup dry white wine
1¾ cups chicken stock
1 bay leaf

1. Preheat oven to 425 degrees.

2. Using chef's knife, cut off top third of each squash. Scrape out seeds and membranes from tops and bottoms. Brush insides and cut edges of bottoms with 1 tablespoon oil to prevent squash from drying out. Place bottoms in roasting pan with ¼ cup water and bake 40 minutes.

3. Meanwhile, remove as much flesh as possible from tops of squash and cut into 1-inch cubes; set aside. If desired, reserve squash tops for later use.

4. Wash and dry bell peppers. Halve lengthwise, core, and remove ribs and seeds. Cut peppers into 1-inch squares. Wash and dry chicken breasts. Cut chicken into large cubes; you should have about 10 pieces per breast.

5. In pie pan, mix together mustard seeds, flour, curry powder, salt, and pepper to taste. Dredge chicken pieces, a few at a time, pressing mustard seeds into meat. Shake

off any excess and reserve dredging mixture.

6. In large heavy-gauge saucepan or Dutch oven, heat ½ tablespoon corn oil over high heat. Sauté bell pepper squares 2 to 3 minutes, or until they begin to brown; remove with slotted spoon and set aside. Add another ½ tablespoon corn oil to pan and sauté onions 1 to 2 minutes, or until they begin to color; remove and set aside. Add ½ tablespoon butter and ½ tablespoon corn oil to pan and sauté half of chicken pieces 3 to 4 minutes, or until firm and golden; remove and set aside. Add ½ tablespoon corn oil and remaining ½ tablespoon butter to pan and sauté remaining chicken pieces; remove and set aside. Remove pan from heat and set aside.

7. Ten minutes before squash bottoms are done, place squash tops, if using, on bottoms and continue to bake.

8. Remove squash from oven. Cover with aluminum foil and keep warm on stove top.

9. Scrape up any burned chicken or mustard seeds from pan, if necessary, and discard. Add remaining 1 tablespoon corn oil to pan and heat over low heat. Add reserved dredging mixture and cook, stirring constantly, 1 to 2 minutes, or until flour begins to brown and mustard seeds begin to pop. Whisk in wine and stock, increase heat to medium, and bring sauce to a boil. Add bell peppers, onions, chicken, cubed squash, and bay leaf, and simmer 10 minutes.

10. Add pepper to taste and simmer another 5 minutes.

11. Remove bay leaf from stew and ladle stew equally into squash bottoms. Cover with squash tops, if desired.

ADDED TOUCH

Apple fans in caramel syrup and heavy cream may sound complicated to prepare but are not. Slice the apples carefully to keep the tops of the fans intact.

Apple Fans

4 medium-size Granny Smith apples
6 tablespoons unsalted butter
¾ cup sugar
1 teaspoon vanilla extract
½ cup walnut pieces
¼ cup heavy cream

1. Peel and core apples. Halve apples lengthwise. Place halves cut-side down on cutting board. Leaving 1 inch at top of apples uncut to hold fans together, cut 5 lengthwise slices in each half. Set apples aside.

2. In heavy-gauge sauté pan large enough to accommodate halved apples, melt butter with sugar over medium heat. Cook, stirring, until mixture begins to caramelize in spots. Add 3 tablespoons water and reduce heat to low.

3. Place apple fans flat-side down in caramel. Increase heat to medium-low and bring to a simmer. Cover pan and cook 3 minutes, or just until apples are tender. Transfer apple fans to serving plate. Press gently to open fans. Add vanilla and walnuts to caramel and cook briefly, stirring, until sauce is slightly thickened. Drizzle sauce over apple fans and top each with 1 tablespoon heavy cream.

Acknowledgments

The Editors would like to thank the following for their courtesy in lending items for photography: *Cover:* plate—Ad Hoc Softwares; bowl—Taitú Uno; spoon—Gorham. *Frontispiece:* pot—Commercial Aluminum Cookware Company; stove—White-Westinghouse; napkin, black bowl—Broadway Panhandler, NYC. *Pages 16–17:* dishes—Dan Bleier; fork—The Lauffer Co. *Page 20:* bowl—Gear. *Page 23:* platter, napkin, glasses, placemats—Gear; servers—Gorham. *Pages 26–27:* platters—Wolfman-Gold & Good Co.; tablecloth, napkin—China Seas; spoon—Gorham. *Page 30:* lacquer bowl and plate—Japan Interiors Gallery; glass—Gorham; tablecloth, napkin—China Seas. *Page 33:* platters, pan, tablecloth—Japan Interiors Gallery. *Pages 36–37:* glasses—Gorham; tureen, bowl, platter, tablecloth—Garnett Brown. *Pages 40–41:* dishes—Leaf-n-Bean, Brooklyn, NY; fork—Gorham. *Page 43:* dishes—Ceramica Mia;

flatware—Gorham. *Pages 46–47:* dishes—Gear; spoon—Gorham. *Page 50:* mat, bowl, plate, glass—Gear; tabletop—Formica® Brand Laminate by Formica Corp. *Page 53:* platter, bowls—Ad Hoc Housewares; copper pan, spoon—Charles Lamalle; tablecloth—Gear. *Pages 56–57:* plates, glasses, coasters—Pottery Barn; flatware—Gorham; tiles—Country Floors. *Page 60:* plates—Wilton Armetale; fork—Gorham. *Page 62:* tureen, platter—Mad Monk; tiles—Country Floors; basket—Be Seated. *Pages 64–65:* dishes, napkin, tablecloth—Ceramica Mia; flatware—The Museum Store of The Museum of Modern Art. *Page 68:* dishes—Eigen Arts; flatware—Gorham. *Page 71:* mat, dishes—Barney's Chelsea Passage; flatware—Gorham; basket—Wolfman-Gold & Good Co. *Pages 74–75:* glass platter—Pottery Barn; ceramic platters—Mad Monk; servers—Gorham. *Page 78:* dishes—Terrafirma; flatware—Gorham; nap-

kin—Pierre Deux. *Page 81:* tiles—Nemo Tile; flatware—Gorham; dishes—Fitz & Floyd. *Pages 84–85:* dishes, napkin, tablecloth—Ceramica Mia; spoon, knife—Gorham. *Page 88:* dishes—Ceramica Mia; spoon—Gorham. *Page 91:* tiles—Country Floors; white platters—Deruta of Italy; servers—Gorham. *Pages 94–95:* spoon—Gorham; dishes—Broadway Panhandler, NYC. *Page 98:* dishes, napkin, tablecloth—Wolfman-Gold & Good Co.; spoon—Gorham. *Page 100:* spoon, glass—Gorham; white plates—Buffalo China. *Kitchen equipment courtesy of:* White-Westinghouse, Commercial Aluminum Cookware Co., Robot-Coupe, Caloric, Kitchen-Aide, J.A. Henckels Zwillingswerk, Inc., and Schwabel Corp. Microwave oven compliments of Litton Microwave Cooking Products.

Illustrations by Ray Skibinski
Production by Giga Communications

Index

103

Time-Life Books Inc. offers a wide range of fine recordings, including a Big Band series. For subscription information, call 1-800-621-7026, or write TIME-LIFE MUSIC, Time & Life Building, Chicago, Illinois 60611.